CASE STUDIES AND PROJECTS IN COMMUNICATION

Neil McKeown

ROUTLEDGE LONDON AND NEW YORK

First published in 1982 by
Methuen & Co. Ltd
Reprinted with revisions 1985
Reprinted 1987

Reprinted 1989
by Routledge
11 New Fetter Lane, London EC4P 4EE
29 West 35th Street, New York NY 10001

Printed in Great Britain by
J. W. Arrowsmith Ltd, Bristol

British Library Cataloguing in Publication Data
McKeown, Neil
Case studies and projects in communication. –
(Studies in communication)
1. Communication
I. Title   II. Series
001.5   P90
ISBN 0-415-04036-1 (pbk)

Library of Congress Cataloging in Publication Data
McKeown, Neil
Case studies and projects in communication.
(Studies in communication)
Bibliography: p.
1. Communication – Study and teaching.   I. Title
11. Series: Methuen studies in communication.
P91.3.M38   1982   001.51   82-7951
ISBN 0-415-04036-1 (pbk)   AACR2

CONTENTS

FOR MY PARENTS

ACKNOWLEDGEMENTS

My thanks for help received before and during work on this book go to the following people (the defects that remain are mine, in no way theirs): Andrea McKeown, for help in every possible way, John Fiske, series editor, to Chas Griffin, Richard Dimbleby, Stewart Marshall, Peter Hartley, Frank Robinson, John Brown, Brian Spittles, Brian Crawford, John Bristow, Bernard Dix, Douglas Pride, Sue Brookes, Allyson Cox, C.R. Hayward, P.K. Kinder, Alan Weir, John Sturgess, to Mike, Danny and Kelly and the Tube Street Gang, for not minding too much when I asked them to go away from the window and play somewhere else; and to all the students who have taught me.

The publishers and I would also like to thank the following for their permission to reproduce material: Macmillan Education Ltd and the Schools Council for Document 1; J. M. Bristow and the Schools Council for material included in Document 2; Gower Publishing for table 2; Elaine Dobney for material included in Document 3; M. Plaskow, the BBC and D. Stuart for Document 4; *The Observer* for Document 5; *The Guardian* for Document 6; Denis MacShane and Pluto Press © Pluto Press for the extract on page 17; the AEB for extracts from the 'A'-level communication-studies syllabus, for Documents 7, 19, 20 and 21, and for diary extracts I and II; Methuen & Co. Ltd for figure 7; the *Media Reporter* for Document 8; the *Leicester Mercury* for Document 9; *Journalism Quarterly* for figure 9; the *New Statesman* for Documents 11 and 12; *Save the Journal* for Documents 13 and 14; the English Universities Press for figure 11; John Mundy, Patrick O'Keefe and Richard Dimbleby for figure 12; Transworld Publishers Ltd for Document 15; British Telecom, publicity division, and R. M. Stanley for Document 16; E. Parsons for organizing the material in Document 16 and setting the case-study questions 1–6 in Assignment L; the Home Office, public relations branch, for Document 17; G. Coward for Document 18; Prentice Hall for figure 18; M. Broome for Documents 22 and 32; D. Brace for Document 23; Alan Ross and the AEB for Document 25; Karen Norton-Spibey and the AEB for Documents 26 and 29; Pergamon Press Ltd for Document 27; Allen & Unwin for Document 28; the BBC and Penguin Books for Document 30; the Federation of Worker Writers and Community Publishers for Document 31; Bharat Parmar and the AEB for Document 33.

N. M.

vi

GENERAL EDITOR'S PREFACE

This series of books on different aspects of communication is designed to meet the needs of the growing number of students coming to study this subject for the first time. The authors are experienced teachers or lecturers who are committed to bridging the gap between the huge body of research available to the more advanced student, and what the new student actually needs to get him started on his studies.

Probably the most characteristic feature of communication is its diversity: it ranges from the mass media and popular culture, through language to individual and social behaviour. But it identifies links and a coherence within this diversity. The series will reflect the structure of its subject. Some books will be general, basic works that seek to establish theories and methods of study applicable to a wide range of material; others will apply these theories and methods to the study of one particular topic. But even these topic-centred books will relate to each other, as well as to the more general ones. One particular topic, such as advertising or news or language, can only be understood as an example of communication when it is related to, and differentiated from, all the other topics that go to make up this diverse subject.

The series, then, has two main aims, both closely connected. The first is to introduce readers to the most important results of contemporary research into communication together with the theories that seek to explain it. The second is to equip them with appropriate methods of study and investigation which they will be able to apply directly to their everyday experience of communication.

If readers can write better essays, produce better projects and pass more exams as a result of reading these books I shall be very satisfied; but if they gain a new insight into how communication shapes and informs our social life, how it articulates and creates our experience of industrial society, then I shall be delighted. Communication is too often taken for granted when it should be taken to pieces.

John Fiske

BY WAY OF A PREFACE:
INTRODUCTORY
CONVERSATION

S: Student   *A: Author*

S Oh, all right then, I might buy it—but what am I supposed to get out of it?

A Well, often the back cover is the best place to look if you want an idea of what a book is about. Or you could try reading this.

S Oh, I never normally read back covers. I often flip through the book though, to see if I like the look of it, and if I don't, then I don't bother. But to tell you the truth, I'm not really all that much used to buying such books, more novels and mags. Still, it doesn't look all that much like an ordinary textbook — especially for 'A'-level.

A Why should it? It's not exactly the same sort of subject is it?

S Well, I don't really know . . . you tell me about it. I'm just doing this communication studies course as a second 'A'-level. I'm not leaving school at the moment, not much chance of getting a job of course, and they said I'd got to have a go at at least two 'A'-levels — said I'd got the ability . . .

A I see . . .

S And as it's a new subject at our place — starting this year — they told us all to go out and buy any cheapish paperbacks we could find on the subject — ourselves, would you believe? Reckon they've got no funds this year for this type of thing.

A Who reckons?

S *They* do, the teachers, that's what I said, isn't it?

A No, it's not . . . . Still, couldn't you get a good idea of what it's about from the cover. Don't you even take notice of front covers?

S Yes, I do, of course I do; but it just didn't seem to do much for me, didn't give me much idea . . .

A Well, what do you expect? It isn't a packet of cornflakes, or likely to be a best seller, you know. And another thing, when a subject's new and growing, like communication studies is, you've got to have some sort of image in order to try and establish the subject.

S Have you? Why?

A At least, that's how the thinking goes . . . . The trouble is, if you make it too jazzy, then the academics and the publishers won't wear it; and if you fill it with too much pure academic theory about communication — like a lot of the American university people seem to — it's bound to put someone like you off, before you've even got into it.

S I see . . . so it goes straight down the middle then?

A Well, more or less; it tries to . . .

S [Thinks] Well, then, it's bound to fail . . .

A Oh, well, we'll see — or would you prefer this approach to the subject, and I quote:

S Oh no!

A Yes, you'll find yourself having to face lots of this during your course, material drawn from different sources:

> Because communication studies is an interdisciplinary subject — what we would call a field of study — students must in their early work spend a fair amount of time familiarizing themselves with 'foundations'; basic assumptions, theories, approaches and concerns of constituent disciplines. Initial study can thus sometimes appear both 'bitty' and over abstract: the student may well feel that time could be better spent in looking at practical examples of communication rather than discussing how best to study such practical examples. Patience is a virtue at this stage, however, for the clarification of such issues can be of great value in the long run. (Corner and Hawthorn, 1980, p. 2)

S Yes, that does sound pretty deadly, doesn't it? And the problem is, I'm not a very patient person.

A Well, if you take that attitude, you're not going to get on very well at any 'A'-level, are you? No, the *real* problem is how you try to clarify communication theory. This book is based on the assumption that the best way to do it *is* to start with particular practical examples from case studies, and to introduce the theory as particular practical issues of communication arise. At the very beginning, just to introduce you to the field, we've included some communication terms and a simple model. In the second half of the book more communication theory is introduced as ideas about student project work are developed. Many of my students have often found it difficult to recall, let alone *apply*, communication theory unless it's closely connected to actual examples of communication.

Instead of just dipping into the book anywhere, though, you should start at the beginning, since the material is supposed to become progressively more difficult. But if on your particular course you are only doing projects and not covering case-study work, then you should start at the beginning of the second half of the book. You should use the assignments included throughout to practise communication skills, and then to apply principles, concepts and models of communication. The first assignment, for example, involves the relatively simple skill of summarizing material; but by the end of the book you should have picked up a lot of help for actually producing a project, which involves a much wider range of skills. You should also, by then, be thoroughly used to reflecting on the *process* of communication as it occurs in your work, and be able to apply the communication models introduced to actual examples of your 'communicative experience'.

S There you go, long-wording it again aren't you?

A Sorry . . .

S Though I think I see what you mean.

A Well, I don't think you can, exactly, until you've actually worked your way through the book.

S Sounds like you're trying to sell me a copy again!

A Yes, and while we're about it, I forgot to mention, regarding the assignments, that the idea is to leave the process of learning from the materials as open as possible. It's up to you to produce your own answers and then discuss them with your tutor and colleagues in class. After all, case-study and project work is essentially social by nature, just as communication itself is. Model answers can tend to prescribe and close down experience too much.

Even when setting up a brand new course at 'A'-level in communication studies, the Associated Examining Board (AEB) refused to publish model answers to case studies. The subject is much more open-ended than many traditional academic subjects — like life, I suppose . . .

S Is the AEB 'A'-level the only course this book is aimed at then?

A By no means, but it's the focus. Every piece of communication needs a focus, or an audience, in mind and a book on such a wide area as this certainly seems to need a focus. It has the same sort of defining effect as the notion of an audience, if you like. But it's hoped this book will be useful for many other courses as well — because students may find themselves doing the same sort of work and needing the same sort of understanding on Technical Education Council and Business Education Council communication-studies courses, in general studies and communication, in adult education, at undergraduate level even — or maybe for no course at all, but just for the fun and interest in it!

S Sounds a bit wide, and a bit vague to me!

A Well, human communication *is* pretty wide. In fact the practical examples included in this book *are* arbitrary. They are only a tiny selection from the infinite range of possibilities in human communication. What has been included here is governed partly by personal and practical factors — like what I as a teacher tend to be most interested in, what material has gone down best with my own students at my particular college in my particular city; and partly by what sort of response I had from other teachers at the particular time I wrote to them and asked if they'd like to contribute material. In a way, communication studies, since it's growing so fast, is still a bit of a 'hit-and-miss' affair, though I hope books like this and the others in the series will help us make progress by clarifying what should be the core skills, principles, concepts and models at this level. But don't expect 100 per cent agreement; there'll still be many disagreements between teachers — it's not like mathematics! And anyway, couldn't you say the choice of one particular novel by Jane Austen for intensive study on an English literature 'A'-level course is at least just as arbitrary?

The idea is that students and teachers can take this book, the materials and advice it offers, as a starting point for their own work in the wide field of communication studies. John Dixon, who wrote a report on English and communication for the Schools Council, pointed out — here's another quote —

S I'm ready this time.

A Somehow, in planning a course, teachers have surely got to take on an independent role, unless, that is, their work, week by week, is simply to be modelled on the specimen papers or on the treatment offered by recommended books (supposing they exist for such a new subject). (Dixon, 1979, p. 88)

And of course, those books simply didn't exist then — they seemed either too advanced or too basic, though the other books in this series are intended to fill some of the gaps.

S Sounds like you're trying to sell me more than one now.

A Not at all. Now here's another short-coming of this one. Don't forget that it's bound to be severely limited by the fact that it *is* a book. More and more projects are being done by students in lots of media other than print: like photography, film, video, tape, tape/slide, etc., but the medium of this one —print—makes it difficult to give examples of the others here. Neither will you find here much information about *how* to operate tape-recorders or video cameras, since that is much better done by tutors and technicians who are on the spot and can help you use particular pieces of equipment. If you're really stuck, refer to manufacturer's instructions!

S Hold on, hold on, what's all this about all this equipment? We haven't even been told yet which teachers are going to take us on this course.

A Don't worry, there are lots of schools and colleges which haven't got a great range of audio-visual equipment, but that doesn't mean you're stuck; you can still learn a great deal about communication. And you'll find out who's taking you in good time for next term, I'm sure. In a new field like this the beauty of it is that there's plenty of scope for initiative in local schools and colleges — and even for you teaching your teachers as you talk to them about your own experiences of communication.

S Teaching teachers! You must be . . .

A I'm not, not at all. Certainly they're more experienced, and have greater powers of analysis and a wider range of skills than you — but how many of them have actually passed the subject at 'A'-level, say? It's an unavoidable problem — it's got to be — but it's got to be faced or no new subject such as this ever stands a chance of getting off the ground. A lot of them will be teachers of English literature by training, but the sort of course you're just starting is going to give you the chance to try a much wider range of writing — and often aiming it at real people in 'real-life' situations — than English literature courses offer: many of these, I'm afraid, are still confined to the essay. Case-study work, for example, can offer you the comparison between a newspaper article, an extract from a novel and a set of photographs, all as aspects of communicating a set of messages.

S You're making it all sound very difficult now.

A Well, it is, quite, but I hope you'll find it interesting and enjoyable, too.

S Well, we'll see, I suppose. From what you've been saying, weren't there any alternatives to producing a book such as this? What could I get that's better value for money?

A Good question, or rather two good questions. Take your last one first. At the present moment, as far as I know: nothing. But in a few years, as work in communication studies develops, or months or even weeks, as printing technology and publishing become more rapid, probably something very much better. And to come to your first point: the next work on case studies and projects might not be a book at all. It might be a set of tapes, or slides, or leaflets, or *really* multi media. And there might then be no real need for a 'national' book like this; it might all get done by teachers and students locally. But now you're already beginning to ask questions about the advantages of one medium over another for communicating a particular series of messages about such work. And I'm beginning to answer them, or trying to, so we're both jumping the gun rather. Let's start about case studies by setting out a few terms and introducing our first communication model.

S Oh all right then, I'll give it a try.

A Good, but just before you really start getting into it, consider these few comments from teachers about setting going such new courses. Go on, then, read on:

What is it that constitutes any discipline? Most fundamentally a discipline is characterized by *an agreed field of study or enquiry*, and is further defined by an *intellectual framework which delimits the questions to be asked.* Information is elicited from the field through a *distinctive mode of enquiry* and the purposes of this enquiry must be *important* or *serious* in ways which need no elaborate justification. Jerome Bruner has also argued that at the core of any discipline lie *concepts* and *principles* 'as *simple* as they are *powerful* which may be taught to anybody at any age in some form.' (Len Masterman, 1980, p. 8)

The teacher might best regard himself as a senior colleague — older and more experienced in analysis — working with junior colleagues, rather than as an expert who will make all the important decisions and through whom all communications will pass. (ibid., p. 28)

I would continue to stress the importance of processes of thought, the need to study the pupils' thinking and look for ways of improving it, as opposed to piling on the data and demanding massive recall; . . . the worry remains that without some interdisciplinary attack, bringing in not only the social-science disciplines but literature and the visual arts — especially the film — and drawing on direct experience wherever possible, the dissociation of 'school work' from 'life' which vitiates much of our secondary education will remain, and the general studies course will be no more than yet another set of games that people play in that curious institution called school. (Robert Irvine Smith, 1968, p. 126)

PART ONE CASE STUDIES

COMMUNICATION STUDIES:
SOME BACKGROUND

1

A first communication model

A simplified linear method of representing what happens in the mass communication process was proposed by Harold Lasswell (1948). His model suggests that we ask the following basic questions of each act of mass communication (e.g. on television and radio or in the press):

	Who	Says what	In which channel	To whom	With what effect
Alternative terms are:	sender communicator actor source encoder addresser	message content	medium method	receiver communicatee audience destination decoder addressee	

Figure 1

3

It will be useful to ask these questions of forms of communication other than mass.

Berlo (1960) defines 'encoder' and 'decoder' thus: 'The communication encoder is responsible for taking the ideas of the source and putting them into a code, expressing the source's purpose in the form of a message. . . . Just as a source needs an encoder . . . the receiver needs a decoder to retranslate, to decode the message and put it into a form that the receiver can use.'

Some communication terms

The use of alternative terms by writers on communication indicates how new the subject is in comparison with others. As study deepens, greater precision in the use of terms is called for: 'channel' and 'medium', for example, have been further distinguished in this way. A channel is a *physical* means of transmitting a signal, including therefore radio, light and sound waves, telephone cables and the body's nervous system. A medium consists of the technology or physical method by which the content or message is changed into a signal that can be sent along the channel. Thus television and radio sets are media; they cannot transmit messages (programmes) to us without the use of the channels of light, sound and radio waves; the telephone is the medium, the telephone cable the channel. One medium may carry to the receiver messages originally sent in another medium. The telephone carries a voice — a medium which is dependent on the physical channels of the nervous system and sound waves. The television set carries a second medium when it shows a feature film made originally for the cinema.

A code includes (a) physical signs that represent things other than themselves (e.g. verbal signs: words and signs based upon verbal signs such as semaphore, braille and morse code); and (b) the rules for *using* these representational signs, and the conventions which decide how, when and where these signs may be meaningfully used to convey messages. People who share a common culture, or sub-groups within the culture, use codes. The physical properties of a channel will thus determine the type of code that can be used in that channel. Since the physical channel of the telephone medium excludes visual signs, the telephone is restricted to the use of words and their emphasis through volume, stress, intonation, etc.

There are two types of 'noise' that can interfere with communication and thus severely affect the meaning that is intended: 'channel' and 'semantic'. Channel noise includes any type of noise that affects the accuracy of the physical transmission of the message. Examples from the mass media include smudged ink in the newspaper due to a fault in the printing process, or interference on a television picture from unsuppressed motor vehicles. Examples from interpersonal communication include somebody speaking over another during a conversation; and from medio communication, a crossed line on a telephone. (For an elaboration of the main types of communication, see chapter 2.) Semantic noise occurs where there is distortion because of the way in which codes are used by the encoder and the decoder, rather than because of the physical nature of interference. The interpretation of the message is therefore not what the sender (encoder) intended.

The message sent to the receiver can also be affected by *feedback*, as the receiver 'feeds' his/her reaction to the message back to the sender. If the person sending the message is a sensitive communicator, s/he will take account of the information s/he gets from the receiver in order to modify aspects of the message as necessary.

Having introduced some basic communication terms and a model, this first chapter includes relatively little by way of communication theory. Most of it is taken up with documents that are the basis for assignments for you to attempt. Your immediate involvement with communication tasks will provide the best basis on which to reflect on the communication process taking place, and thus build your later understanding of communication principles, concepts and models.

This chapter also attempts to give you a general picture of some of the background to the relatively new field of communication studies by presenting material that focuses on why and how things are changing in language, literature and communication studies in our schools and colleges. The material included concerns developments that have given rise to the sort of communication studies course you are likely to be following. It is drawn from a variety of sources that use a variety of channels, codes and media to produce messages aimed at a variety of audiences. While undertaking case-study and project work you will be involved in a much greater range of channels, codes and media than are employed in this book, whose message is inevitably determined to a certain extent by the limitations of its medium: print.

DOCUMENT 1

Extracts from a survey that investigated reasons why students are taking communication studies courses

We shall begin by taking a sample of more than a hundred students in the first year of their course (AEB 'A'-level in communication studies) and asking what they hoped for and wanted from it. Their perceptions at this stage offer another guide to the aims in the process of realization.

'I wanted to do something new.' 'It is a challenge.' Not every student will be prepared at 16-plus to opt for what may look like a totally new subject. For those who do, that sense of breaking new ground (and knowing that your teachers are doing so too) may itself be a stimulus. In communication studies the territory is not altogether unfamiliar, but the idea of studying it systematically is an extension beyond any previous course. 'I thought it would open up as wide and varied a field as possible.' 'Many 'A'-level subjects are specializing in one particular area . . . . I chose this course because of its broadness.' 'It seemed a very wide subject, which I could later on choose one aspect of perhaps, because I'm not sure exactly what I want to do.'

We have already noted the major recommendation that courses at 'A'-level, while allowing for early specialization in some cases, should also be providing for a delay in specialist choice. If communication studies combines a broad offering with the possibility of developing specialist interests later in the course, this is a major contribution to fulfilling such recommendations. The question is, how will teachers develop a course that meets the desire to 'broaden my knowledge' while at the same time ensuring that 'a student can concentrate on those areas that interest him most'? In some ways this seems to call for new forms of group work or individual assignments.

There were other indications that students would differ both in what they might well contribute to the course and what they might be relating communication studies to in the rest of their work in college or school. 'It was an obvious choice with English literature and film studies', wrote one student. Indeed in our sample, English literature is the 'A'-level most likely to be taken in association with communication studies. But there are other and different possible associations. 'Chosen to help further my knowledge of the background to art work, i.e. how we are affected by visuals.' 'Seemed to offer a practical supplementary study to my other subjects — sociology and political studies.' 'A useful subject to combine with my languages, French and German.' In addition, though they were not represented in our sample, we have been working with one college where the majority of students were taking science 'A'-levels. (Dixon, 1979, p. 71)

ASSIGNMENT A

(Document 1)

Communicator
1. Explain briefly, giving reasons, who you think the 'we' in the document is.

Audience
2. Explain briefly, giving reasons, at whom you think the document is aimed.

Context
3. Explain briefly, giving reasons, where you think the document was first published.

Content
4. Summarize in not more than 150 words the message contained in the document.

Layout
5. Given the audience at whom you believe the document is aimed, suggest possible ways of setting it out more clearly by changing punctuation, paragraphing and sentence order.

DOCUMENT 2

Main reasons for choosing the communication studies course

The following comments by students, made half way through their first year, offer some insights into their motivation and interests:

WHY?

'A challenge, as I wanted something different from the ordinary courses available.' 'Different to all the previous subjects I had taken.'

'Relevant to everyday life.' 'It seemed a relevant subject in that it deals with the role of the media in our lives.'

'Useful subject in any job.'

'Fits in with other 'A'-levels, e.g. social sciences, all of which inter-relate.'

'Run in conjunction with psychology and sociology and is described as a "social behavioural course".'

'Greater understanding of the way in which society works.'

'It should mean that I can express my ideas clearly.' 'Helps me improve my own communications.'

'Many 'A'-level subjects are specializing in one particular area; the communication course covers such a wide area that a student can concentrate on the sections which interest him most.' (From the Schools Council Survey, 1978)

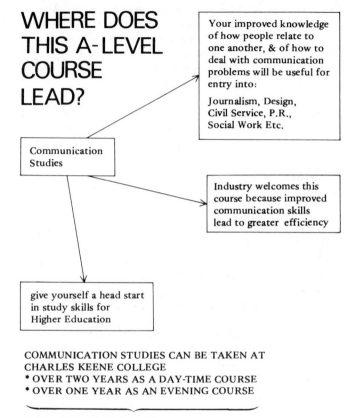

WHERE DOES THIS A-LEVEL COURSE LEAD?

Your improved knowledge of how people relate to one another, & of how to deal with communication problems will be useful for entry into:

Journalism, Design, Civil Service, P.R., Social Work Etc.

Communication Studies

Industry welcomes this course because improved communication skills lead to greater efficiency

give yourself a head start in study skills for Higher Education

COMMUNICATION STUDIES CAN BE TAKEN AT CHARLES KEENE COLLEGE
* OVER TWO YEARS AS A DAY-TIME COURSE
* OVER ONE YEAR AS AN EVENING COURSE

starting SEPTEMBER 1979/
enrolment 4th & 5th Sept.

DOCUMENT 3

What is communication studies — and why you should choose it!

As second-year students who have just completed the two-year 'A'-level course in communication studies, we thought it would be a good idea for us to try out our communication skills on *you*!

We want to tell you about this subject, what it is about, and why you should study it!

There are many sections to the course, but speaking from experience of the work we have covered, let's try to outline it this way:

Case studies form one part of the course. Case-study material can be newspaper articles, pamphlets published by firms, or even photographs. There is a three-hour exam; two days before this exam you are given selected material to study; you then have three hours to show that you can complete various communication tasks, using the material. You might have to write letters or memos, or design a photographic exhibition or publicity posters. And you have to show you can deal with communication problems in life by putting yourself in someone else's position.

In the second year you have to do a *project* on a topic of your choice. This is internally marked and externally moderated, and there is a final oral examination too. Last year's subjects ranged from the Phoenix Theatre to a guide to Asian customs; from a guide to the YHA to a booklet for staff at Sainsburys!

Then there is a *'theory' written exam* which is itself split into four sections:

(a) the *development of communications* — roads, railways, newspapers and broadcasting, etc.:
(b) *mass communication* — how the mass media affect people's lives and the changes that happen in society;
(c) *means of communication* — dealing with how we communicate with each other; and lastly,
(d) *theories of communication* — in which models of communication are analysed and assessed, and their usefulness considered.

This is basically the syllabus — but why choose to study these things? Most of the work can be related to life — understanding people, the way they act, how publicity works, what body language is. You begin to see that TV programmes have different meanings, newspapers have specific audiences and styles, and you begin to understand why. The subject is basically about everything that influences you, whether it is the mass media or this notice.

And how you could improve this notice!

ASSIGNMENT B

(Documents 2 and 3)

Communicator
1. Explain briefly, giving reasons, who you think has written each leaflet.

Audience
2. Explain briefly, giving reasons, at whom you believe each leaflet is aimed.

Context
3. Suggest where each leaflet might have been made available to its audience to have maximum impact.

Content
4. Summarize in not more than seventy words the message contained in each leaflet. List any words, sentences, phrases which are not clear to you. Suggest reasons why this is so.

Layout
5. Given the audience at whom you believe each leaflet is aimed, produce an improved layout for each leaflet (on A4 paper).

DOCUMENT 4

Basis for a radio script

maurice plaskow is the schools councils curriculum officer i asked him why do teachers find it so difficult to teach their sixth form pupils english i dont think they find it difficult to teach them i think that the dilemma that many teachers are in is that their own experience of english and therefore the tendency of many of them in their own teaching relates to a time when sixth forms were devised for a very small proportion of the pupils who were going on to further and higher education that is no longer the case and i think the big problem thats facing the 16–19 year old group is that weve got to redesign courses that will be seen to be more appropriate to the needs of the student and bearing in mind that only a proportion of that group will be going on into higher education well whats wrong with the present teaching method it is based by and large on an english literary tradition that is to say most english courses for advanced level of the gce are still essentially english literature courses one of the central messages that comes through this report that the schools council has published today on english 16–19 is that the way forward is in one of its strands and probably a strand that will be seen to be relevant to a lot of these young people is to redesign english to embrace english and communication bearing in mind for example that a great deal of the input to use the jargon for young people is not just literature but the whole world of media teachers have to take into account that young people receive information and experience through tv through radio through their own kinds of literature and not just through printed texts so that english is communication on a much broader framework yes you used the word receive there yes but what about their ability to communicate themselves right i think that this again has to be expanded not just limited to the response through a conventional essay in written form and one of the exciting developments has been through pupils development of oral skills that is to say their ability to communicate in oral language as well as their abilities to communicate through just these media that is to say through making audio tapes and indeed their own tv programmes as a means of making statements and their own communication which isnt necessarily through the medium of print but to what extent has this method been tried and tested oh quite widely now a lot of courses have been devised to take this in perhaps more particularly and this is another point that comes out strongly in the report on further education further education is perhaps further on because the restructuring of their courses has happened more quickly through the new technician and business education courses theyve had to look more closely at ways of introducing courses to their clientele which is of course even more widely spread than the schools because these are children very vocationally orientated but do you expect the end result of such a method to be well received by the employers yes i do because i think employers will see the relevance of this to their needs because they are not terribly interested in receiving young people who have had a heavily literature based course they want young people who can communicate both with their employers and with their clients that is to say who have

confidence in oral skills language being able to talk being able to formulate ideas and thoughts themselves so that they can communicate them and also to be able to absorb a lot of information and pull it together and then make sense of it so that i think employers will also see it as more relevant to their needs and when is it all going to come into effect well its happening now what we hope is that the report will accelerate the thing very considerably.

ASSIGNMENT C

(Document 4)

(You should work in groups of at least four students.)

1. Each student should read the document. The group must then reach agreement about the number of communicators involved in the communication.
2. The group should then *prepare* the document so that it can be used as the script of an interview on a national radio programme. You will need to agree on the punctuation necessary and rewrite the document accordingly.
3. The group should then *present* the interview with a student playing the role of each communicator. Those who are not playing roles should evaluate the

effectiveness of the presentation, taking particular note of:

(a) the appropriateness of intonation, pausing, use of non-verbal communication (gesture, facial expression, etc.);

(b) how effectively the communicators are communicating with each other;

(c) how effectively the communicators seem to be communicating with the stipulated audience;

(d) ambiguities and inconsistencies in the original document and the extent to which these are removed by the performers;

(e) the extent to which repetition, hesitation, change of direction in mid-sentence, interruption, the use of colloquial language, aid, or interfere with, effective communication.

4. Your group should now *discuss* any changes in punctuation or wording which would be necessary to change the document into the text of a feature article appearing in a national education journal. Emphasis should be placed on the differences between spoken and written language.

5. Lastly, each member of the group should give examples from the text of each communication term introduced so far in this book.

This material focuses on changes taking place in language, literature and communication studies in our educational institutions. But what are the social changes taking place in Britain that give rise to such changes in education? The views of Professor Edmund Leach (then Provost of King's College, Cambridge) on these social changes appear below. This article was printed in the national Sunday 'quality' newspaper *The Observer*, 20 February 1977.

DOCUMENT 5

PRIVATE LINE
Edmund Leach

Literacy be damned

So after all, despite our vastly increased national expenditure on education, academic standards are falling; half the school-leaving population is illiterate; and so on and so forth. This chorus of old-fashioned Whigs, from Annan to Boyson and right on through the alphabet, certainly provides food for thought, but I am sceptical.

I hold it as self-evident that the content of education changes with fashion and that such changes reflect a positive adaptation to shifts in the structure of society. As the young Marx put it: 'In every epoch the ruling ideology (*Gedanken*) is the ideology of the ruling class.' For more than a century it has been accepted as dogma that proficiency in the basic skills of reading, writing and arithmetic is the necessary foundation for any form of universal school education, but this antiquated fetish was linked historically with the rise of industrial capitalism and the epoch of European colonial expansion, so perhaps it may be on the way out.

Let me throw a few stray facts into the cauldron.

(a) It seems very likely that Homer could neither read nor write.

(b) There have been many wide-ranging and highly sophisticated political regimes which got along very nicely without reading, writing or arithmetic – the Peruvian Empire of the Incas for example.

(c) Educated human beings of one sort or another must have been around for 50,000 years or more but most of the languages which are today recognized as suitable vehicles for primary school education were only committed to writing less than a century ago.

This operation was the work of Christian missionaries who believed that in order to achieve personal salvation it is necessary to read the Bible. The practical effect of such education was to destroy the existing indigenous arts and crafts, which the schoolchildren concerned might otherwise have learnt, and to produce a superfluity of cheap clerical labour for the white colonialists.

(d) Electronic calculators which can perform all the operations that the average school leaver is expected to understand can be bought for less than the price of half-a-dozen visits to the cinema or a dozen pints of beer.

(e) Tape-recorders and typewriters provide a much more efficient means of recording speech than any form of calligraphy (either shorthand or longhand).

(f) Signatures can be forged; thumbprints can not.

(g) The skills of shorthand and typewriting are palpably more useful than the ability to write longhand. But what proportion of school leavers have been encouraged to learn either?

(h) Written texts, whether in books or in documents, tend to be valued because they can be made unambiguous. But this specious clarity is achieved only at great cost. Since the real world of experience is not one-dimensional and linear, it follows that by gearing our whole educational system to the written word we automatically teach our young to misinterpret their environment.

(i) Laboratory monkeys quickly learn to recognize the scenes that they are shown on a TV screen and the judgments they make about such scenes seem to be very like human judgments.

This surely has implications for human education? Why be complicated when you can be simple? When we listen to speech we decode directly the message received through the ears; when we observe the world we decode directly the message received through the eyes. But if I write a letter I first have to think in words and then transform those words into sensitive movements of my fingers. Conversely when I read a letter I must first transform a visual message into an aural message 'in the mind'. No doubt it is very remarkable that we are able to do this, but the acquisition of such skills is in itself very much a circus trick which has no special merit except perhaps that it gives us a comfortable feeling that we are superior to monkeys.

Today, when tape-recorders, TV screens, radios, electronic calculators and computers are so readily available a great deal of this effort is quite unnecessary. A few centuries from now the study of twentieth-century alphabetical texts will have become the quaint specialism of a few learned academics, the equivalent of the tiny coterie of present-day scholars who can read ancient Egyptian in its cursive hieratic form.

Let me be more positive. If it is true (which I rather doubt) that among the school-leaving population a general competence in the three Rs is on the decline, this may be because the young have a clearer under-standing than their elders both of what is available and of what is worth while in their cultural environment. Reading, writing, and arithmetic are still basic skills if you want to end up as a synthetic member of the nineteenth-century liberal middle class or as a still more synthetic member of the nineteenth-century Whig aristocracy, but these categories no longer represent 'the ruling class', and the associated cultural values (despite their continued gross over-representation in the school curricula) are no longer the dominant cultural ideology.

On a world scale, *all* information which is conveyed in normal linguistic form, either in speech or in writing, is socially divisive; it favours those who speak that particular language as their mother tongue and excludes all the rest. By contrast, information which is conveyed in non-verbal visual form — e.g. as traffic signs, silent cinema, silent TV, or in special 'international' symbolic languages such as that employed in mathematics, is socially cohesive — it draws African, Asian, European and American into one world.

The art of writing started out as a secret code through which a literary elite exercised bureaucratic control over the illiterate masses. Later, when literature became internationalized as a channel of communication, the medieval literati, both in Europe and in Asia, had the good sense to operate with a very limited number of much simplified languages. But then came the Fall. Gutenberg gave us the fruit of the Tree of the Knowledge of Good and Evil. As the printed word proliferated we became more and more aware of how different we are; today there are the literate Saved and the illiterate Damned, but even among the Saved we go out of our way to be mutually incomprehensible.

Literacy, in the form in which we at present know it, does not deserve its status as the sacred cow of basic education.

(*The Observer*, 20 February 1977)

ASSIGNMENT D

(Document 5)

1. Summarize, using not more than 200 words, Leach's argument in the *Observer* article 'Literacy be damned'.
2. Assume that this same argument has to be presented to an audience of 16-year-old school leavers with Certificate of Secondary Education (CSE) passes in mathematics and metalwork but no examination passes in either language or arts subjects. You may not use more than 250 words to present Leach's message but you may add as many illustrations or diagrams as you choose.

Discuss in groups the following:

3. Can a school student make full use of an electronic calculator without first appreciating the nature of the mathematical tasks that need to be completed?
4. Is it possible to master shorthand or typewriting without first being able to read print and to write fluently in longhand?

Audience, medium and message

Professor Leach also stated his views in an address to a national conference of the Association for Liberal Education (ALE) and the script of his speech was later published in their journal, amounting to an article of much greater length. Why did he change the medium for, and the length of, the presentation of his views?

He wanted to get the widest possible total audience for his message, so he used all three channels open to him: the speech, the article in the ALE journal, and the *Observer* article. In modifying the length of his message to each medium, he inevitably modified slightly the *content* of his message.

The great advantage of the *Observer* article was that, though brief, it reached the widest audience, since the paper's readership is numbered in hundreds of thousands. Thus the message would here have been *broadcast*; not all of the paper's readers would have bothered to read his article, and a good proportion of those who did might have been only half interested in it.

The audience at the ALE conference would have numbered only tens. His message here would have been *narrowcast*; but the great advantage for the communicator, Professor Leach, here, is that probably 100 per cent of this audience would have been interested in his message. Response in the form of questions and comments — *feedback* — from his audience would certainly have been immediate, and would probably have been much fuller than for either of the printed versions.

The published feedback to the *Observer* article consisted of just four brief letters in the following week's edition (though other responses may have been forwarded to Professor Leach by the editor).

The advantage of writing the ALE journal article was that Professor Leach knew he could thereby reach a wider audience than the conference provided. Further, it would have been a fairly receptive audience, with a high proportion of people both informed about his topic and interested in fresh views on it.

Each means of communication carries with it advantages and disadvantages. It is the purpose of case-study work to develop your appreciation of these, and to select appropriate means.

Examinations and skills

Document 6 summarizes the conclusions of a Schools Council report on the value placed on exam qualifications by employers. Advice then follows on how to develop two central skills: summarizing texts and writing press releases. Next comes an assignment that attempts to link these skills to some of the theoretical considerations introduced above and to other possible elements in your communication studies course (e.g. the local mass media). It is this type of learning, involving three elements simultaneously, that is likely to be most productive.

Summarizing texts

When writing a summary you should attempt to use the following method:

1. Skim through the whole of the passage to give yourself a general idea of the ground it covers.
2. Read the passage carefully.
3. Re-read the passage noting on a separate piece of paper, or marking on the passage if permissible, the key words and phrases that carry the main points in the passage.
4. Write a rough version of the summary, writing complete sentences around your key words and phrases.
5. Word count the rough summary to ensure that it is approximately the length required.
6. Check through the rough summary for expression, paragraphing and punctuation. Ensure that the language and style you have used are appropriate for the purposes of the summary. Amend as necessary.
7. Check the rough summary to ensure that it contains all of the main points from the original passage. Amend as necessary.
8. Word count to ensure that your summary is the length required.
9. Write out a neat and accurate final copy.

If you lack the time to carry out all of these steps you should decide, before attempting the summary, to omit step 2.

Exams 'over-valued' by employers

By John Fairhall, Education Editor

Public examinations can give only a rough approximation of a pupil's achievements, a Schools Council report states. Exams are being over-valued by employers and it is time that they and the public generally accepted their limitations.

About 30,000 different GCE and CSE syllabuses are being studied by pupils in this country, and the Schools Council's Forum on comparability has been attempting to find out if it is possible to compare results.

How does a grade C in French from one board compare with that of another, or with grade C maths or yet another subject with a Mode 3 teacher-set exam?

Their answer is: only very broadly and imprecisely. The chairman of the forum, Mr Peter Dines, said that the limitations of public exams were particularly marked with exam papers which allowed a choice of questions. Two pupils could get the same grade in the same subject after being examined on different skills.

The forum's report says there is growing demand for more precise comparability of grade standards in public exams, but there is tension between this pressure and the existing curricular freedom given in schools. Whether the two can be reconciled, says the report, is a matter for the policy-making bodies, not for the forum.

The alternative might be much more uniformity in examining.

There is not even a straightfoward comparison between subjects, the report says; one 'O'-level exam entitled English could be very different from another with the same title.

The decentralized nature of education in this country adds to the difficulties of achieving comparability.

'The amount of curriculum development which takes place, the freedom given to teachers in this respect, the existence of several independent examining boards and the response of the boards to teachers' wishes, all contribute to a curricular diversity which is reflected in the examinations . . . .

'This variety of syllabuses and styles of examining, with little common core and little coordination, makes it difficult to compare grade standards in terms of quality of work.'

On grading, the report says that definitions of grades in GCE and CSE may be of limited value.

On 'A'-level grades the boards employ a mixture of judgments of the quality of work and statistical information, including guidelines such as the expected 70 per cent pass rate . . . .

'Standards in public examinations: problems and possibilities.' Schools Council Occasional Paper 1
(*The Guardian*, 18 December 1979

How to write press releases

The following advice is based on that given by MacShane (1979) in his very useful book *Using the Media: How to Deal with the Press, Television and Radio.*

A press release is a partially digested helping of news, which can easily be made into the real thing by the professional journalists in a news room. News editors and journalists like press releases: they save work . . . . A press release is in all its forms essentially a news story. Whether a two-line announcement about a new appointment or a ten-page account of a complicated report, the press release has to obey the basic rules of news writing. The first rule learnt by every trainee journalist is to concentrate on 'the five Ws': *What, Who, Where, When, Why?* Every press release should begin with *four* Ws, and you should start off by writing: *What is happening; Who is doing it; Where it is happening; When it is happening. What, Who, Where, When*, do not have to be in that order, but they should always be in the first sentence or two of your press release . . . . The fifth W is *Why* something is happening. It is necessary to explain the reasons behind, or causes of, the situation that justifies producing the press release . . . . The first sentence or two — in journalists' jargon, the 'intro' — can be the key to the success or failure of the press release . . . the intro *has to contain the most interesting fact* about the issue or event . . . . Essentially a story is being told — much as you would give a factual report to a meeting. *Concentrate on facts* . . . in descending order of importance . . . . Information and views should be presented, in a *clear, digestible form* . . . for the kind of press release intended for the majority of the media — the regional evening papers, weekly papers, local radio and local freelance agencies — the *terse economical style* of the news stories in the *Daily Mirror* is worth aiming at. Keep sentences short. A maximum of twenty-five or thirty words will do. (pp. 70–3)

ASSIGNMENT E

(Document 6)

1. Summarize Document 6 using not more than 150 words.
2. Apply Lasswell's model of communication to Document 6. Identify, with a brief explanatory note, the following elements in the article: 'sender', 'message', 'receiver', 'channel', 'effect'.
3. John Fairhall may well have used a press release from the Schools Council when writing his article. Write a press release, aimed at your local newspaper, covering any recent event that has occurred at your school or college that was ignored by the newspaper but which you feel should have received coverage.
4. Consider, in terms of its audience, why your local newspaper does not give greater coverage to events at your school or college. It will be necessary to collect data on the readership at whom your local

newspaper is aimed (the circulation department of the paper is a possible source).

5. If it proves difficult or impossible to collect such data, write a report analysing whether your problems arose from your own shortcomings as a researcher/ interviewer/communicator, or from the possibly confidential nature of the information itself.

6. You should discuss the way particular information you may discover about your local paper relates to other aspects of your course, e.g. mass communications.

Audience: the traditional literary view

The material and Assignments I have used so far emphasize how differences in audiences for messages necessitate different presentations of the message. The concept of audience is central to project and case-study work in communication studies.

Most 'A'-level English literature courses ignore this concept. Hoggart (1970), however, suggests that these questions should be asked of literature: What are the audiences for different forms of literature? What are the audiences for different levels of approach? What are the different expectations and backgrounds of audiences? Can the average audience today be said to comprise 'intelligent laymen', 'common readers', or what?

Traditional literary criticism neglects such questions, emphasizing instead that 'A'-level English literature, for example, allows deep personal qualities to develop in the student. Indeed, precisely because the student is writing in relative privacy, his or her feelings can become that much more refined, delicate and sensitive than if s/he were writing for public consumption.

Traditionally, too great an emphasis has been placed on those elements of our culture that are restricted in their use; and too little emphasis on the popular. Such emphases in literary studies have much in common with the attitude Roszak (1970) attacks when writing of those who are criticized for trying to make aspects of Oriental culture more widely known in the West:

> Too often such aristocratic stricture comes from those who have risen above popularization by the device of restricting themselves to a subject matter that preserves its purity only because it has no conceivable relevance to anything beyond the interests of a small circle of experts. (p. 133)

Of course, at 'A'-level, the study of literature has not attained such heights; those tend to be found mainly within our institutions of higher education.

Communication studies and the tigers

Communication studies courses are more likely to be useful to that overwhelming majority of students who do not intend to make a career out of teaching English literature. The forms of writing involved here are not restricted to the essay for a private audience, and in case-study and project work students can be encouraged to make use of their own social and work experiences. The hint is dropped here, for example, as a student on such a course explains why he selected the project topic that he did:

> Deciding on a subject for the project was easy — having worked as a clerical officer for a year after leaving school in the Department of Health and Social Security (DHSS), I had often thought how poor the leaflets that the government produced were in explaining Supplementary Benefit, and upon the need for some leaflets in Asian languages. The office in which I worked (Newarke Street) has a higher proportion of immigrant claimants outside Brixton than any other office in England. The need for some leaflets which explained Supplementary Benefit in a simpler form in Asian languages as well as English, seemed to fit the need for communication studies well.

This remark by a student about his own work emphasizes the close relationship between the worlds of study and work.

The innate conservatism of much teaching and many teachers — a conservatism now being shaken by the forces unleashed by Britain's relative economic decline — is well illustrated in a fable recounted by Peddiwell (1939). The fable is the motif for his book *The Sabre-tooth Curriculum*:

> A prehistoric tribe intended to educate its children by teaching them particular skills necessary for their survival. It was decided to make the first subject 'fish-grabbing with the bare hands'; the second 'woolly-horse-clubbing'; and the third 'sabre-tooth-tiger-scaring-with-fire'. The objectives were to enable the children to survive by catching food, providing themselves with clothing from the horse's skins and giving security by frightening tigers away from the tribe's water.

> Later a new ice age descended on the tribe's living area. A glacier began to melt into the tribe's stream making it difficult to fish in the muddy water and impossible to catch them when they darted behind boulders brought down by the glacier. Subsequently the woolly horses died out and the tigers moved away, their place being taken by antelopes and bears. However, the original skills were still being taught to the children back in the schools.

During the last half-century many English literature courses, particularly in higher education, have earned their places in *our* sabre-tooth curriculum, though many teachers have argued strongly for changes in content and the way in which the subject is taught. Communication studies does appear to be more relevant now than literature courses to many student needs. Should its advocates forget, however, that the antelopes and bears will one day disappear too, then these courses will also become part of a sabre-tooth curriculum.

AN INTRODUCTION TO CASE STUDIES

2

Setting the compass

The first chapter of this book draws attention to some of the factors behind the recent development of communication studies, introduces some basic communication terms, and initiates some practices. Chapter 2 introduces case-study material, some communication principles, and methods for learning from your practice.

We should see case-study material in the first instance simply as data — the raw material from the real world which involves human beings and institutions in the process of communicating. Our understanding of communication principles and practices will be based on an analysis of these materials. As the material we look at becomes more complex, so do the principles that will be dealt with.

We cannot hope to cover all of these principles in detail for two reasons. First, a book of this length simply does not offer sufficient space. Second, understanding of communication principles cannot fully develop aside from their practice. They cannot be learned abstractly. The principles you will become familiar with from working through the material included here should, however, enable you to deal with more complex material independently.

The process of description in any field cannot begin until the field is first divided—somewhat arbitrarily it may appear—into separate areas. It is impossible to describe or comprehend the entire field at once. When the different areas have been identified and understood in some detail they can then be related to each other again, and our understanding of the field consequently deepened. This first stage appears to deny that the areas are connected, but our developing understanding brings together these different areas and confirms the relatedness of the whole field. Similarly, with the division of knowledge and understanding into different subjects at, say, GCE (General Certificate of Education) 'A'-level: the events of the real world studied in sociology may be the same events, viewed from a different perspective, covered in history or touched on in a novel studied in English literature.

For principles and models of communication to be fully understood they must constantly be related to the data of the real world, actual acts of communication involving human beings or institutions.

We shall approach case-study material by looking first at some relatively simple material: ten photographs (Document 7).

These photographs are an example of a purely visual case study. They were drawn up by the AEB for 'A'-level communication studies; there were other examples from the AEB that I considered using in this book, but they were unsuitable because of the book's format. The content is here affected by the medium I am using to present my message. I am using

DOCUMENT 7

the medium of *print*, but it is possible that in the near future students might be presented with a cassette tape-recording of case-study material, or a tape-slide sequence, rather than a book such as this. You should therefore consistently attempt to consider the relevance of the advice given here to case-study material presented in other media.

Case studies: limits and fits

On the AEB 'A'-level course — which we shall take as a focus for case-study and project work — the students received a booklet containing these ten black and white photographs (A4 size) two days before the examination. They would then either receive another case study in addition; or during the three-hour exam would have a choice of questions to answer on the one case study. They were not permitted to talk about the subject with their teacher(s) but they could discuss it with anyone else (students, friends and relations).

The exam questions were designed to give students the chance to show that they could:

(i)   Examine content analytically.
(ii) State the results of their analysis in a suitable form, e.g. statements; articles; letters; reports; charts; diagrams; algorithms; tables; captions.
(iii) State the connections between style, medium, content and intention.
(iv) Detect and describe inconsistency, inaccuracy, redundancy, or incompleteness in verbal, graphical and statistical material.
(v)   Put themselves in the place of another person in a clearly defined situation and produce material which will reveal the ability to suit style, method of presentation, and content to a given recipient.

(AEB syllabus, 'A'-level communication studies)

During the two days the students had the material they could apply their understanding of communication principles to it, even though they did not know what the questions in the examination would be.

Analysing to some purpose

How does the student go about 'examining content analytically'? Analysis is always easier if there is a known *purpose* to the analysis. The problem here is that at this stage the student does not know this purpose. What is s/he going to be asked to do with the material? Of course s/he should make notes on it, for it is the *process* of making notes that is valuable.

What happens when you make a note? You select the significant item from the mass of material that surrounds it. In the case of the ten photographs, significance/meaning is relatively difficult to deal with. Most of us are simply not used to making notes on pictures; rather, we tend simply to look at them. For the analysis to get off the ground, we would have to have some *standard*, some *criterion*, by which to select what is significant and therefore worthy of note. It will be productive, then, if we have a *purpose* in mind when we analyse material. (We should note here that 'purpose' is one feature omitted from Lasswell's model. His omission has been criticized by other writers. You might now find it valuable to add the concept of 'purpose' to his model and to re-apply it to some of the documents included in chapter 1.)

Symbols, significance and meaning

We tend normally to associate 'significance' and 'meaning' closely with *verbal* significance and meaning.

Words are the most explicit and precise symbols we use in communication, but by no means the only ones. We live in a world of symbols. We have agreed that the marks made thus: 'DOG' on a piece of paper, for example, represent a hairy, usually domesticated, quadruped. Anyone who uses the marks 'PENCIL' to refer to the same creature is excluding themselves from the communication process. They could only communicate with others if they could get them to agree that these marks stand for this creature, for there is no *necessary* connection between the symbol and the creature referred to (the *referent*).

'In one form or another, symbols are always overt; they must be seen, heard, felt, or smelled. They condense abstractions into delimited objects.' (Hoebel, 1966). They are the bricks with which the structure of human communication is built, involving 'the transmission of information, ideas, emotions, skills, etc., by use of symbols — words, pictures, figures, graphs, etc.' (Berelson and Steiner, 1964).

Visual images such as photographs are likely to suggest a much wider range of possible meanings to the receiver than verbal symbols. Any words that accompany the photograph, or the context in which it appears, may be used by the communicator to guide the receiver towards the preferred meaning. During work on this case study (Document 7) the student has to establish a *preferred* reading out of a number of possible ones and arrange the photographs so as to lead the reader towards it.

Whatever problems some people might have in seeing that there is any significance at all in photograph 6 — this particular picture symbol — *you* have a distinct advantage. You are a member of a specified audience for the ten photographs; you receive and look at them in a particular way because you are to use them in an academic course — a very different way from the way it would be if you merely saw them scattered in the gutter. Due to the *context* in which the photographs are presented to you, and the absence of explicit verbal symbols accompanying them, you yourself tend to invest the photographs with significance. You *search* for it. You will assume that they have not been selected at random since you know they have to be used for particular communication purposes. Your problem if presented with highly verbal material would be of a different kind. Such material would contain very many *explicit* meanings and your task in this case would be to select those you think would be most relevant to your demonstration of the above-mentioned abilities.

Looking for significance

Taking this relatively simple example of the photographs, you might now find it useful to look at them individually and ask yourself what *qualities* they demonstrate. You could present the information for your own future reference as in figure 2.

The following comments are intended to provide guidelines for making notes on the case-study material and to develop your appreciation of the photographs.

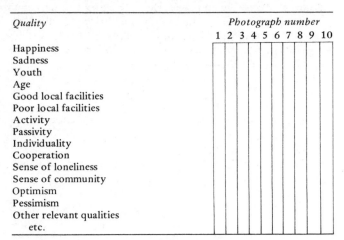

| Quality | Photograph number |
	1 2 3 4 5 6 7 8 9 10
Happiness	
Sadness	
Youth	
Age	
Good local facilities	
Poor local facilities	
Activity	
Passivity	
Individuality	
Cooperation	
Sense of loneliness	
Sense of community	
Optimism	
Pessimism	
Other relevant qualities etc.	

Figure 2

Consider the use of the medium of photography in our society. For what purposes are series of photographs commonly used? (You should not assume that you will be required to use them all throughout all of the tasks.) By whom are such series of photographs frequently used? When? How? Who is (possibly) using these photographs to say what, to whom, and with what effect? And for what possible purpose? Put as many of the photographs as you can in an order that tells a story or delivers a message. Supposing you can use all of them, and the order is: 1, 5, 7, 3, 9, 8, 2, 4, 10, 6; look at the sequence carefully, then look at the individual photographs. Note the particularly significant features in each that enabled you to fix it in the appropriate place in your message. What other significant features are there in each photograph that could suggest a different message?

You 'know' from your own experience that in our society (though not necessarily in others), dogs are often used as substitutes for human companions. Thus it is relatively easy for us to arrive at the equation: man plus dog = man minus family/friends. You bring your social experience to the photograph and from this mix significance emerges.

Now concentrate on each of the photographs individually in turn. Take photograph 6. Just now this photograph appeared differently since it was part of a message that had a meaning. If you describe it to yourself as 'a photograph of a lonely old man with a dog', you are *investing* the photograph with meaning. The signs that suggested this title to you were partly in the picture itself. But they arise partly too from your own *feeling* that these signs in this context could represent loneliness. To somebody from a different society, unfamiliar with walks, dogs, parks, and loneliness, the photograph simply would not suggest this meaning. If in your story you want to use this photograph to emphasize a feeling of loneliness, it might be a good idea to place others near it which you feel highlight the same feeling. But simply because you have invested the ten photographs with one message, the sequence does not have to remain so.

Make notes on the features of all of the photographs that helped you develop a story from them, and then alter the sequence to construct a second story. Note how, as you construct your second story, the meanings you attached to the photographs in order to make your first story tend to cling to the photographs. Your primary meaning, for example that photograph 6 evokes loneliness, clings to your secondary meaning. But your primary meaning disappears as your secondary meaning comes to the fore and you construct your second story. For example: you might have decided that the old man and the dog live near the flats shown in photograph 3, and that rather than depicting loneliness, photograph 6 now indicates the relative affluence and calm of retirement when compared with the very poor play facilities available to the girls outside the flats. On top of a story or a message the possibility of a wider theme — the conflict between youth and age perhaps — has emerged. And other themes will follow as you work through the many possible different sequences for the photographs. *Meanings are in people not in words:* and not in photographs.

'Telling a story' is a basic method we regularly use in order to produce significance. If we wish to understand an aspect of our experience, we turn it into a narrative — we select and connect elements in a way that 'makes sense'. In this respect, the message from the photograph consists of a system of signs/symbols in a particular combination that produces meanings for you *as a result* of coming into contact with you, a particular individual living at a particular time in a particular society. You bring aspects of your experience to the photograph, reacting to the signs/symbols and codes the photograph carries. Not every candidate working on this case study will see the same significance in each photograph, the same possibilities of meaning; and the range of offered answers will be correspondingly wide.

A straight communication model

This description of what is happening in the process of communication appears closer to reality than descriptions that confine themselves to a purely linear representation of the process, such as Shannon and Weaver's (1949) model

(figure 3). This view represents the message in the photograph as objectively there to be simply transmitted to you, the receiver, who awaits its reception. In this view, the receiver is largely passive and contributes little to the nature of the message itself. Barriers to communication ('noise') may occur, however. An instance here would be such poor quality in the printing of the photograph that a significant detail (the old man for example) is imperceptible. In this view, the reprinting of the photograph to the same standard as the others (the norm) would remove the barrier to communication. The emphasis throughout is on the sender as the conveyor of the message rather than on the *process* of interaction between photograph and receiver which results in significance.

As we saw earlier, the significance in a photograph is much less explicit than the significance carried by verbal symbols. As Leach (1976) puts it:

> The grammatical rules which govern speech utterances are such that anyone with a fluent command of language can generate spontaneously entirely new sentences with the confident expectation that he will be understood by his audience. This is *not* the case with most forms of non-verbal communication. Customary conventions can only be understood if they are familiar//A private symbol generated in a dream or a poem, or a newly invented 'symbolic statement' of a non-verbal kind, will fail to convey information to others until it has been explained by other means. This shows that the syntax of non-verbal 'language' must be a great deal simpler than that of spoken or written language. (p. 11)

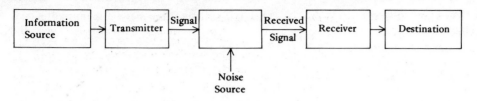

Figure 3

The photographic material in this case study, which carries in itself relatively little meaning, will be invested with extensive verbal meaning by you as you carry out specific tasks.

When you have made thorough notes on the photographic material you should generalize your understanding of the medium of photography by consulting theoretical writings such as those by Berger (1972), Evans (1978) and Fiske (1982).

You should repeat this process as you do case-study work: constantly attempt to relate your own practice to the reflections of others engaged in similar practices in the same medium.

Predicting the future

You should next attempt to produce a list of questions that you deduce you are likely to be asked about the material, referring to the range of skills that you will be required to demonstrate when doing case-study work. If you know the approximate number of questions you will be asked, you should attempt to produce at least twice as many.

If you remain content with less you may well get yourself into a narrow way of thinking.

You may be asked to use the material in a particular role. If you construct only a few questions you may find yourself tied to the roles those questions produce and find it difficult to adjust to performing the role that is actually required. The aim of this exercise is not to help you predict the questions. This is a practice which is all too often indulged in as a substitute for real learning—a practice brought about primarily by the examination system. Rather, the objective is to help you familiarize yourself as fully as possible with the material in the time you have available.

Then, of course, you should attempt to answer some of the questions you or your colleagues have constructed. Compare and criticize answers. The learner becomes the teacher: and the teacher the learner.

The questions which were actually set for the above material are reproduced in Assignment F (though you should not yet attempt them!):

ASSIGNMENT F   (Document 7)

Leisure facilities

Your school has decided to support a local campaign for the improvement of facilities for games and general leisure activities in your area. You have been given ten photographs by the secretary of the school's photographic society and asked to prepare a variety of drafts, using the photographs to support your writing.

1. Reject any photographs you do not think could be used to support the campaign and produce a letter to the secretary giving your reasons for not using them.
2. Put all photographs in a sequence and write captions on them such as would appear on a display in the local library.
3. The local newspaper is going to carry an article on the problem. Select two photographs that you think could be used and write captions that would arouse sympathy for the campaign.
4. Prepare an article of 300 words for the school magazine outlining the problems and the lack of facilities. Select three photographs that would support your unbiased, informative article.
5. Write a formal letter to the local town council asking for permission to present your case at the next meeting of the sub-committee dealing with leisure facilities. State how long the presentation will last, what facilities you will require and the main points you wish to make.

(AEB specimen case study)

The next part of this chapter deals with the concept of *audience* by considering how best to tackle questions 3 and 4. What are the characteristics of the different audiences at whom we shall be aiming our separate answers to these two questions? The concept of an audience is central to communication studies. That is why we deal with it at some length here, and consider the main issues of the audience before we deal specifically with the two questions.

Let us first consider more generally how different types of audience may be distinguished by considering different types of communication. Then we shall look at problems of communicating with different strata within the same audience.

What are the general characteristics of audiences for the following types of communication: 1) interpersonal, 2) mass, and 3) medio?

1 *Interpersonal communication* can be defined as face-to-face communication between two or more people, where all of the senses can be used. The communicators are close to each other and there is the possibility of immediate feedback. In a conversation between two people, if X gives information to Y and Y receives some of it but is unclear about some aspect of it, then Y asks X a question to clarify the area that is unclear. This is *feedback*, since the knowledge that Y has not understood part of the message assists X in formulating all or part of the message. This process can be diagrammatically represented as in figures 4 and 5.

(a)   X selects objects on which to base his message from the infinite number available to him:

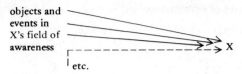

objects and
events in
X's field of
awareness

X

etc.

Figure 4

(b) X sends a message about the selected objects and events to Y and Y produces feedback to X:

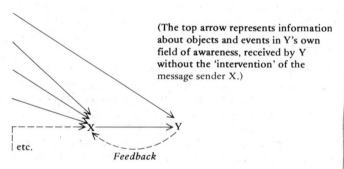

(The top arrow represents information about objects and events in Y's own field of awareness, received by Y without the 'intervention' of the message sender X.)

X → Y

etc.

Feedback

Figure 5

In fact most interpersonal communication is very much more complicated than this example indicates. It does not simply consist of communicators sending information by means of explicit verbal symbols to each other, but also of a

complicated encoding and decoding process. Verbal symbols are only one code.

Schramm's (1955) model (figure 6) can thus be applied to interpersonal communication.

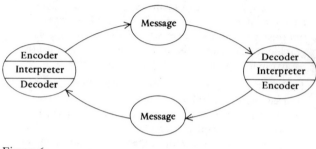

| Encoder |
| Interpreter |
| Decoder |

Message

| Decoder |
| Interpreter |
| Encoder |

Message

Figure 6

2 *Mass communication* involves the public transmission, by means of a technology, of messages from complex institutions, to large, relatively anonymous and heterogeneous audiences. The messages often involve considerable expense, are aimed at the biggest audiences possible, often simultaneously, and typically are in a disposable or non-permanent form (though modern methods of copying, storage and retrieval can increase permanence). Mass communication thus tends to limit the number of messages that can be transmitted and severely limits and delays the possibility of feedback between sender and receiver. In our society at present the owners of the technology and the 'experts' who work full-time for the owners, tend to have the dominant say in selecting which messages shall be transmitted to the mass audience.

3 *Medio communication* lies between interpersonal and mass communication in character. A technology is used, but only under limited conditions, and not to communicate with the large anonymous audiences at which mass communication is aimed. In medio communication there may be only one receiver; if more, those taking part would usually be known to each other and not anonymous as in mass communication. The common forms in our own society are, of course, the letter and the telephone.

Thinking about audiences

Into which of the categories of communication do the audiences we have to aim at in questions 3 and 4 — the local newspaper readership and the school magazine readership — most closely fit? Let's take the first criterion: the *size* of our local newspaper audience. If you want to check the latest circulation figures for local or national newspapers, consult Hartley (1982), *The Media Reporter* (quarterly), or *Benn's Press Directory*, which can usually be found in the reference section of local public libraries. Your local newspaper will obviously have a smaller readership than a national, but will it be more or less homogeneous than that of a national? The motive that leads most people in X-town to read the local newspaper is their common interest in events that have taken place in X-town. Although differentiated by income, occupation, status, leisure activities, and so on (i.e. social class and taste), most of the citizens of X-town momentarily ignore these differences in favour of their common interest in local events. This, indeed, is one way in which a local newspaper's influence can blur class and/or social tensions. (Such a

— *The way they communicate to different (types of audience)*

comment on influence would be unlikely to be made by someone who subscribes to the view that communication consists simply of the transmission of messages.) Some local newspapers exert additional influence due to the monopoly position they hold in the area. While community and alternative newspapers have developed recently in many towns, they have rarely challenged the established local paper, which may well be backed by the financial resources of a national newspaper chain, or by other business interests. The 'degree of expense' involved in acquiring the professionalism and expertise to rival the local newspaper on its own terms, has often been simply too much for the alternative papers.

In contrast, the readers of national newspapers are not united by any community, local or regional interest. It is an educational or literacy level, a social or political outlook, social class or a leisure interest, that unites the readers of the *Daily Mirror* and distinguishes them from the readers of *The Times*.

What are the essential characteristics, on the other hand, of the school magazine audience? Surely it is closer to the local than to the national newspaper audience in character? The common interest of people in this audience is the school they attend. Their age range as an audience will, of course, be much narrower than either of the two newspaper audiences. As you clarify the nature of these two audiences remember that you probably *know* far more about your school audience, since you are or have been a member of that community. It is essential when doing case-study work, that *in every case*, before attempting to carry out the task, you spend time clarifying for yourself the characteristics of the audience specified.

Let's now consider the different audiences for each of our five questions: for question 1 the audience is the secretary to the school photographic society; for 2 it is the visitors to the local library (i.e. members of the local community who have a stronger than average interest in reading books and newspapers); for 3 it is the people in the community who buy the local paper (as discussed above); for 4 the audience is the pupils at your school who read the school magazine; and for 5 the members of your local council who are on the sub-committee dealing with leisure facilities.

Photographs tell stories

Let us now consider how these concepts of audience work out in practice by tackling question 2. Here our task is to 'Put the photographs in a sequence and write captions for them such as would appear on a display in the local library'. What will be the characteristics of the audience for such a display? We can assume that the audience will live in the catchment area that the library serves; we can therefore assume that most of our audience will know the local area with which the campaign is concerned. For example, we can assume a familiarity with the street names, and with some of the areas photographed. We can assume that most of the audience will know the level of facilities provided in the area, and that many will have views as to whether these facilities need drastic improvement or not. Some of our audience may believe that facilities previously provided have been abused and be against the provision of more; a reminder that our audience will not necessarily be homogeneous by age or social class, though if drawn from one relatively uniform housing area, it could be homogeneous by class.

We are asking here questions about how our average audience member is likely to *decode* the message we have *encoded* in the captions. What prejudices, habits and pre-dispositions are likely to make them *interpret* the verbal symbols in our captions in one way rather than in another?

Since our audience knows the area, we should make sure that our captions make explicit points about the campaign, points which remain only implicit in the photographs. In no sense will our captions be effective if they merely tell our audience what it can already *see* for itself in the photographs, or what it already *knows* about the area.

Remember that we have to use all the photographs and that some will be more obviously useful to our purpose than others. Photograph 4, for example, apparently poses some immediate problems. Ignore difficult elements such as this for the moment, and work to the following scheme: (a) take the most useful photographs for our purpose (say, 2, 3, 5, 7, 8, 9 and 10) and state briefly your message around these; (b) put them in the order which presents that message most effectively and persuasively to the audience; (c) only now should we consider what we can make of the 'difficult' photographs (1, 4 and 6) and consider how we can include them in our message. We should not substantially alter, though we may slightly modify, our message to make use of these photographs. We should attempt to use these 'difficult' photographs to *reinforce* the meaning in our message.

Context affects content

We now have a pretty full idea of what our audience, purpose and message are going to be. But in order to communicate to the maximum effect we have to ask ourselves some questions about the *context* or setting in which the communication is to take place. How long can we expect our average audience member to spend looking at the display? This should help us determine the length of the captions we have to write. How are the *physical constraints* of the local library likely to affect the size of the display and the order of the photographs? What will be the most appropriate height at which to mount them? Should we put one caption beneath each photograph, or allow one caption to cover two or more photographs? Should we play safe here in interpreting the question and necessarily assume that 'write captions for them' demands one for each? How do we ensure that our audience is attracted to the display? Is there one particularly eye-catching photograph that could be placed at the beginning of the display and used to attract attention?

Our first caption might need to introduce the theme to our display, and our last to summarize it. Do they? Do our captions bring out, and add to, the meanings implicit in the photographs? Our captions should never merely describe what is evident in the photographs, though they may be used to clarify any ambiguous features.

ASSIGNMENT G

When you have considered these points (and any others that your class discussion concludes are relevant) you should:

1. Put the photographs in sequence and write captions for them.
2. Consider to what extent the following captions fulfil the above requirements.

(a) A lick of paint, some litter-bins, and a watchful eye from the park-keeper would make all the difference to the existing Brook Street play facilities.

(b) Looking for a safe place to play. Mark and Mandy Woodfield are a danger at present to themselves *and* to the general public.

(c) Extra noise for the residents in the flats — and a danger to themselves. Surely these children from the Brook Street area deserve a better future?

(d) It *can* be done by our town council. Saturday-morning action in Western Park on the other side of town.

(e) Deprived — but making the best of it. Four-year-old Matthew and brother John play on the waste ground near Brook Street.

(f) How much better are facilities for the old in this area? But the deprived young citizens of today are tomorrow's adults.

(g) All smiles at the moment — but these children in

the derelict houses on Willow Street could so easily find themselves in trouble with the law.

(h) Don't! That's the answer six-year-old Gary Baxter is getting at present — but the best answer for everybody is to provide him with somewhere safe and convenient to play.

(i) Another shot from Western Park. There children are scoring every time, because the council provided these facilities years ago. But why can't all parts of our city be treated equally well?

(j) Can we ignore little Jyotika? She's still too young —like so many other children in the area—to know where it's safe to play, or to ask for what she really needs.

3. Using these captions, arrange the photographs in any sequence you choose to convey a message suggested by the captions.

4. Diagrammatically represent the relationship between the five different audiences, using no more than twenty words to accompany your diagram.

These captions attempt to establish a direct, familiar and colloquial relationship with the audience, in the hope that the sense of participation evoked will lead to audience support for the campaign to achieve improved leisure facilities. The appropriate relationship to the specified audience can be established only when you have firmly grasped the purpose of the communication, the nature of the audience, and the characteristics of the role you have been asked to play in dealing with the case-study material. The relationship must be carried through consistently and imaginatively once it has been decided upon; and imagination will be needed in deciding what the relationship is like. Provided it is consistent with, and aids the development of, your theme, it is acceptable for you to invent and include any extra information that will give a feeling of authenticity to your communication. You must be particularly careful here, however, to ensure that none of your invented information in any way contradicts or reduces the impact of the information you are given in the original case-study materials.

Where we are

The relatively simple case-study material above, in a single medium, has been taken as the basis for the introduction of additional communication terms and the development of skills. On completion of the Assignment you should summarize in note form the terms, principles and models of communication that you have acquired so far from this book. You should compare your summary with summaries made by other students in your group. Reflecting in this way on your experience of learning is one of the essential methods by which you will become increasingly sensitive to human communication.

When completing your summary you were involved in a fourth type of communication, 'intrapersonal'. It is such communication that will form the basis of the project diary/report that will be covered in part two of this book.

CASE STUDIES: BEYOND SKILLS

3

Barnlund (1968) has pointed out that:

> The encoding-decoding process that occurs while a man waits alone outside an operating room or introspects about some personal tragedy is a sufficiently distinctive type of communication to require separate analysis. For this reason it is desirable to restrict 'intrapersonal communication' to the manipulation of cues within an individual that occurs in the absence of other people (although they may be symbolically present in the imagination). As such, its locus is confined to a single person transacting with his environment. (p. 8)

You are practising intrapersonal communication about human communication already. The necessity is to become increasingly conscious of this practice. One focus for such consciousness is the project diary/report covered in chapter 6; others are the devices offered in the next chapter in which we tackle increasingly complex case-study material requiring more extended work.

Types of case study

This chapter begins by trying to indicate the range and types of case-study material you are likely to meet, some of the communication principles and models their study gives rise to, and the types of skill you will need to develop. It is not possible in a book of this length to include material that exemplifies *all* of the principles, models and skills relevant to a communication-studies course, so use this book as a handbook; it can point you in the right direction for further study; and use the bibliography for further guidance.

The term 'case study' sometimes mystifies, but in itself the term is relatively unimportant; what is more important is the *process* of studying communication. This process cannot develop abstractly, but only as we deal with increasingly complex materials. In chapter 2 we dealt with a relatively simple type of material. In this chapter more complex materials are introduced, followed by a commentary on them and assignments for you to tackle.

Let's try to classify the different types of material we are likely to meet, and the different areas of learning to which they give rise.

Table 1 *Case-study chart*

Nature of content
Level of case-study material
Length of learning process
Number of media involved
Type of media involved
Skills needed
Role play performed
Communication principles developed
Relevant communication models
Strengths revealed
Weaknesses revealed
Relevant further reading
Relevant further practice
Tutor's assessment
Self-assessment
Reasons for self-assessment

On finishing each case study you should complete as many of the sections in table 1 as you can. In this way your understanding and self-assessment of the processes of communication in which you are involved will be consistently developed.

Keeping a log of the case-study material you deal with should help develop your consciousness of communication. It should also help you to move from practice to theory. It should serve as a reminder, for the purposes of revision, of the approaches, skills, principles and models most relevant to particular types of material. And lastly it should provide you with a means of assessing your own progress, preparatory to keeping a diary/report on your later project work. The essence of such work is self-activity by you, the student, and this can only take place fruitfully if you prepare and organize yourself for it. The case-study chart should help you to do this.

ASSIGNMENT H

Use the case-study chart (table 1) to classify your approach to the photographic material dealt with in chapter 2.

Selecting and reporting

Let us now look at some case-study material that raises questions concerning practices and processes in one area of the mass media — the press. Document 8 is an extract from an article, by the editor of a weekly provincial newspaper, which appeared in a specialist quarterly aimed at media practitioners (the *Media Reporter*, 1, 3, 1977). The author reflects on the way in which race relations are reported in the British press and makes some recommendations. Document 9 includes (a) a report in a local newspaper of a development in race relations; and (b) an editorial article from the same day's edition expressing an opinion on that development.

DOCUMENT 8

Race relations — news or non-news

by J. Clement Jones

A well-known editor looks at an area in which he finds the media at fault

We are a multi-racial society. In fact we have been so for some time, however much many natives of the British Isles may dislike the thought. This fact is, I feel, too often over-looked by many colleagues in the media who go on treating race as high-priority news. We still think of race and race-relations stories in the 'Man Bites Dog' top news category, when this is not really so. So often we see the same old stereotypes, the same old situation-stories — which would probably have been spiked if they had not had some racial connotation — brought up to lead or near-lead status. Since we are already a multi-racial society they do not really merit that space.

I am not advocating the suppression of any story just because it has either overtones or undertones of race. But I believe that a great deal of what is treated as news about race is no more relevant than the fact that we are also a multi-skilled and multi-cultural society. But so long as we in the media go on acting as if race is top priority news, the public will believe this to be the case. And in our dealing with race as part of our watchdog role, we are often guilty of the grave sin of giving greater prominence to events, not causes. We often suppress, though not always intentionally, the causes of conflict in favour of conflict itself.

I believe that in our continued attitude to race as top priority news, when it no longer is, we are guilty of several sins:

1 We often make the bullets for racists to fire; and we then sit back and acclaim their hits, but not their misses.

2 We have made race and colour prejudice synonymous terms.

3 We stereotype. White society in the UK has come, largely through us, to expect a certain type of behaviour from anyone whose skin pigmentation is different from our own, and we perpetuate that belief.

4 We have not bothered to learn about the ethnic minorities in our midst — where they come from, why they have come, what they believe in, what are the reasons for their cultural differences both from us and for the differences which exist among themselves. We take refuge in saying 'They all look alike to me' and of course *post hoc* ... they all are alike.

5 We seldom report racial matters constructively and objectively.

Suppression, as I have said already, will get us nowhere. Apart from the fact that it would be morally wrong, it would lead to even greater distrust of the media than unfortunately already exists. That any mistrust should exist in the first place is our fault. We have only ourselves to blame for the fact that at no other time in the history of mass communications has the credit rating of the media been lower.

We are to some extent ourselves the recipients of the same kind of stereotyping, which we apply to others in race matters. There is hardly an educationist, an academic, a professional man or a person in a responsible position in industry, who has not at some time or another taken a side-swipe at the media for its alleged irresponsibility. Sometimes it is justified. There are times, however, when it is not justified, and we feel hurt by their stereotyping us. But do not let us aggravate the situation. Let us try to retrieve something. And one way which I would suggest is by taking a more responsible attitude than we do to race-relations reporting.

Various terms have already been bandied about — Conscious Editing is one; Positive

Editing is another. Though what is meant is quite clear in the minds of those who have coined the terms, they have already been perjoratively used by others who have not wanted to accept them. They have been held by some of these people to be contrary to and a betrayal of press freedom. My favourite composing-room overseer had a riposte which very expressively said what I think about that. So instead of using either term I am going to add a third. I am going to define it. It is 'Sensitive Reporting and Editing'.

I have chosen the word 'sensitive' carefully, because I think that despite the multiracial nature of our society, and what I have said about non-news, it *is* a sensitive area. And in case someone is wanting to catch me out on an apparent contradiction, I add that a sensitive area is not necessarily a newsworthy area. In speaking of race as a sensitive area, I mean that it is one where prejudice is still rampant: one in which many people apply to events criteria which are far more emotional than the criteria they would apply to similar events in a non-racial context; one in which consequences of a story are quite unpredictable, because we only see the tip of the iceberg of racial prejudice; one in which, if we stopped to consider the lessons of history (and I do not mean just Hitler and the Jews), we might realise what an uncharted mine-field we are treading.

. . .

People of good will and who should be intelligent enough to know better, still conveniently make the media the scapegoat for all that is wrong with society. Recently, there has been a spate of books and pamphlets sponsored by the race-relations industry attempting to show how biased and racist the media generally is. Most of this research is done by people who do not know how the media functions, and they do not bother to find out before they start their work. Moreover, most of their research is desk and library work. It is very easy to sit down with a batch of cuttings, most of them with banner headlines, and to draw critical conclusions from them.

Of course it looks bad when such material is taken out of context of the total news picture of the day and without inner knowledge of what went on in the various newspaper offices concerned at the time. Newspapers are fair game for this sort of monitoring because, compared with the electronic media, it is so much easier to do. So far as I know, no one has sat down with a full month's tapes of half-a-dozen local radio stations and assessed their coverage, particularly their handling of race matters in 'phone-in programmes. I doubt anyone has the required stamina! To the extent outlined above the race-relations industry can often be biased against and unfair to newspapers.

On the other hand much of the criticism has been justified and I would not attempt to defend it. The main criticism has been of our stereotyping. No pun intended, but two blacks do not make a white. If our critics stereotype us, it is no justification for us to stereotype them, or anyone else.

There is strong and justified criticism for our predilection for conflict or strife reporting; for our habit of dealing with results and effects and not with causes; for letting inaccuracies and lazy reporting go unchecked; wrong use of the word immigrant is a typical example; for seemingly allowing the National Front and similar groups to manipulate the media; for giving J. Enoch Powell an inordinate amount of publicity for utterances which in essence have always been predictable and repetitive since his 'rivers of blood' speech.

Few newspapers today are journals of record. The proliferation of courts, council committees, statutory bodies, miscellaneous tribunals and other pressures on staff and space make news handling an extremely selective and subjective matter. Enough editorial material is thrown away and stories left uncovered to have filled the newspaper over and over again. There is now a great contradiction between those who want publication, warts and all, on the one hand and on the other sensitive reporting, sensitive editing, and more time devoted to producing rounded and more responsible stories.

Except for a few which have been able to move successfully into the age of high technology, most of our newspapers are still printed by the principles introduced by William Caxton whose quincentenary we have recently celebrated. Technologically we desperately need to move into the new era to survive. I would suggest that we also desperately need to re-think some of our editorial principles. Far too little thought has been given to this side of newspaper production. We still go on doing the same old things in the same old way, because they have always been done like that. Is it too much to hope that a closer look at our coverage of race will lead to a radical reappraisal of our role?

Clem Jones was editor of one of the biggest evening papers in Britain, the Express and Star, Wolverhampton, when Enoch Powell was a controversial resident and MP.

DOCUMENT 9

NO VIGILANTE GROUPS IN LEICESTER - ASIANS

ASIANS in Leicester are "unlikely" to heed the call of some London immigrant organisations to form self defence groups, community leaders insisted today.

They believe that the tensions which have divided communities in the East End of London and Walsall, and the lack of confidence in the authorities to tackle the mob violence, do not exist in Leicester.

Yesterday in London the leaders of three reputable national Asian organisations urged their people to form self defence groups in the face of increasing "Nazi" violence.

The statement, issued jointly by the presidents of the Standing Conference of Pakistani Organisations, the Federation of Bangladeshi Organisations and the large Indian Workers' Association in Southall, said they were filled with horror and dismay at the "increasing acceptance of racialist and Nazi views in Britain as manifested by the escalating attacks of physical violence upon defenceless citizens of Asian origin."

Part of the statement said: "For the past decade, the Asian welfare organisations have resisted pressure in encouraging their members to join self defence

...● See leading article—Page 12

vigilante groups in the face of such attacks and in spite of considerable apathy from the supposed forces of law and order. We now believe that the time has come when we must urge our people to look to their own defence."

Dr. A. F. Sayeed, president of the Standing Confederation of Asian Organisations, said he did not take the suggestion seriously. He thought that it was a "gut reaction to a tense situation".

Expressing a personal view Dr. Sayeed said: "I do not support the idea of vigilante groups. But the National Front and other racist groups cannot be ignored. Unless the authorities take effective measures to stop these attacks it will be difficult to prevent these groups from forming."

"The activities of the National Front are becoming so prominent that the law and order situation is beginning to break down in these areas."

He did not think that the groups would challenge the police. He thought that the groups, if formed, would be based on small clubs.

Dr. Sayeed felt that so much could be lost if vigilante groups were formed. "I think these groups will become alienated not only from the Asian community but would lose the sympathy from the host community."

Mr. Tara Mukherjee, president of the Confederation of Indian Organisations in the U.K., who lives in Leicester, said he sympathised with the anxieties of community leaders but thought it was unwise to form unofficial groups outside the perimeter of the law.

Mr. Mukherjee said his organisation had written to the Home Secretary, Mr. Merlyn Rees, imploring him to visit the troubled areas.

So far this has not been taken up, although the chairman of the Commission for Racial Equality, Mr. David Lane, and the Bangladeshi High Commissioner have visited the strife areas.

Mr. Mukherjee said: " We are opposed to the forming of vigilante groups by any ethnic minority group.

"It is the job of the Home Secretary, the police and the local authority to deal with an issue of law and order."

He did not think vigilante groups would be formed in Leicester.

"Leicester is far more peaceable than other parts of the country. It is unlikely that racial violence would flare up on the scale of Wolverhampton and London.

"In Leicester we have got a spread of the Asian community. There is no kind of ghetto in Leicester where communities are huddled together and are the subject of attacks.

"It would be very difficult to create racial violence here in Leicester. The relationship between non-whites and whites is far better than in many parts of the country."

● Mr. Mukherjee heads a delegation to meet Mr. William Whitelaw, Shadow Home Secretary on July 19th, to outline their views on immigration into Britain.

Front page lead story, 15 July 1978

Leicester Mercury

at St. George Street, Leicester
LE1 9FQ. London Office: 44 Fleet
Street, EC4Y 1BN.
Leicester 20831.

PEACEFUL PROTECTION

THE calm advice of Asian leaders in Leicester is reassuring in the face of extreme views being expressed by reputable community leaders in parts of London.

Inter-racial tension has led to fear among members of Asian communities in some suburbs, with the unfortunate result that there is now a call for self-protection bands to be raised.

It is understandable that people under pressure should feel that whatever protection they are given is inadequate. It is a man's instinct to defend his family and his property with every means at his disposal.

But the call reported on Page One today must not be heeded.

The Asian leaders in Leicester wisely realise that over-reaction is a deadly danger. If one section of the community bands together to resist their enemies, the other side will escalate their efforts. The result: trouble in far greater degree than would ever have happened if trust were placed in the forces of public protection.

The police have been underpaid and overworked to the point of scandal. But now the issue of law and order is being given top political priority.

Given the resources to do their job, the police will protect the public. They have proved this over and over, and the Asian leaders in Leicester are to be commended for their faith in them.

But far more important than any law-enforcement agency is the good sense and goodwill of ordinary men and women — regardless of colour or creed. For they realise that here in Leicester our strength is in the willingness to accept differences and get on with the business of living in peace.

Editorial
article,
15 July 1978

45

ASSIGNMENT I
(Documents 8 and 9)

1. Describe, in about 100 words, the nature of the audience for whom the newspaper editor, Jones, might have been writing the article in Document 8.
2. List the criteria Jones puts forward for judging what is normally 'newsworthy'. Why does he suggest a modification of such criteria when reporting race relations?
3. What possible barriers to communication exist between 'men and women of sincerity, intelligence and good will' on the one hand, and 'responsible newspaper men and broadcasters' on the other? What are the possible sources of these barriers? (For a checklist of barriers to communication, see chapter 4.)
4. Evaluate the extent to which the front-page lead story from the *Leicester Mercury* (Document 9a) is an example of the type of reporting recommended by Jones.
5. Evaluate how and to what extent the 'editorial comment' in the *Leicester Mercury* (Document 9b) attempts to influence the reader's opinions about race relations.
6. Summarize the distinction between what Jones refers to as 'a journal of record' and the modern newspaper.
7. What implication is carried by the use of the term 'race-relations industry' in the first article?

When you have completed Assignment I you should complete the case-study chart (table 1). (A master copy of the chart should be drawn to a size which comfortably allows you to include all the information you will want; a number of copies should then be run off. Ask your tutor if s/he can assist by giving you a banda so that multiple copies can be printed. These can then be filed together by you and completed in the form of a diary/report of work done and progress made.)

For another view of the treatment of racial conflict by the mass media and some alternative recommendations for reporting, see Hartmann and Husband (1971). You should read and make notes on their systematically set-out article, even though the facts on which it is based are now dated. A fuller application of the same sociological technique to the television news coverage of industrial relations is given by the Glasgow University Media Group (1976).

Perceiving and selecting: a model

The process of selection begins, however, prior to the act of communication. It begins as the events of the world are perceived, as the model by Gerbner (1956) modified by Fiske (1982) (figure 7) indicates.

Gerbner has defined human communication in general as social interaction through messages. Such messages, such communication events, take place within a shared common culture.

Though more complex than Shannon and Weaver's, Gerbner's model remains fundamentally linear in its approach, rather than circular. But it differs from Shannon and Weaver's model in that it makes a connection between the 'message' itself and the real-world event that the message is about.

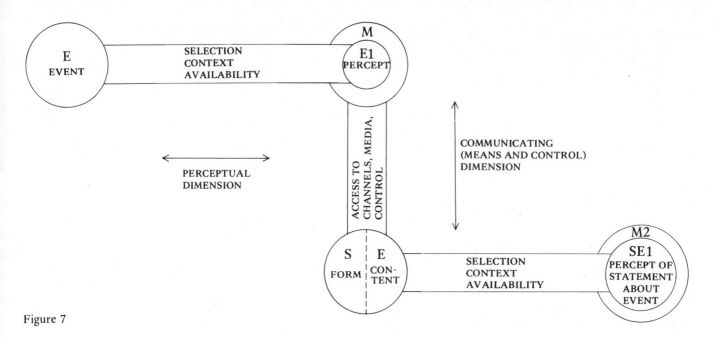

Figure 7

Note
(i)   The movement in this diagram is from top left to bottom right.
(ii) Horizontal movement ⟷ represents the *perceptual* dimension.
(iii) Vertical movement ↕ represents the *communicating* dimension.
(iv) M = Sender of message;   (v) M2 = Receiver of message.

Further, it sees the process of communication as consisting of more than one aspect. Gerbner describes first the perceiving/receiving process through which the event is brought to our attention (the first horizontal arm); and second, the communicating process itself, through which we attempt to convey the message to the receiver (the vertical arm).

Gerbner's model postulates an event E, perceived by a person M. The event as perceived, E1, is the result of perceptual activity by M, affected by what M is, his own inclinations, consciousness and intentions, and by the context in which he perceives the event. For example, the Wolverhampton *Express and Star*'s editor, Jones, may perceive an event, a speech on race by Enoch Powell. Jones's perception of this event may be affected by (a) the fact that personally he may be tolerant towards coloured people; (b) his intention to promote peaceful race relations through his newspaper; and (c) the fact that the speech may have a major impact in Wolverhampton, Powell's constituency.

In perceiving E, Jones attempts to marry, consciously or not, the external stimulus of the speech to his own internal thought and concept patterns. Perception is also a matter of culture and attitude. These factors produce the modification from E to E1.

The way in which the statement about the event is presented (the vertical arm of the model) is the result (i) of the media available (e.g. speech, film, photograph, print, etc.) and (ii) of the rules and conventions which, in our society and culture, govern the use of such systems.

In this model, SE is what we normally call a message about the event (Shannon and Weaver's 'signal'). The statement about the event is further distinguished. The choice of the best medium through which to present the message (whether speech, film, photograph, print, etc.) is a fundamental problem for the communicator. The given message, E1, can clearly be communicated using a number of different media. Jones could have decided to deliver his message about the reporting of race relations by addressing a meeting of the National Union of Journalists (NUJ) instead of writing it for publication. And having chosen to write and print it, as an editor himself he was able to choose between national, local and specialist newspapers.

The medium selected will, however, affect the content of the message, since the relationship between the two is dynamic rather than static. Had Jones chosen to write his message for publication in a national daily tabloid newspaper, the length, words, tone and structure of the article would have differed.

Selection in the vertical arm is as important as in the horizontal. A signal about E1 cannot be complete and unaffected by form, any more than E1 can be a complete reaction to the original event E.

The vertical arm includes the question of who has access to the mass media and influential channels of communication in our society. Here, the opportunity to suggest how race relations should be reported is given to professional media practitioners and public figures, rather than to the average member of the newspaper reading public. The former have the time, facilities, status and 'expertise' to present such views, whereas the latter typically do not.

In the next stage of the process, the second horizontal arm represents the reader's reception of the article in the *Media Reporter*. M2, the receiver of the message, reads the article containing Jones's views. This perceptual activity by

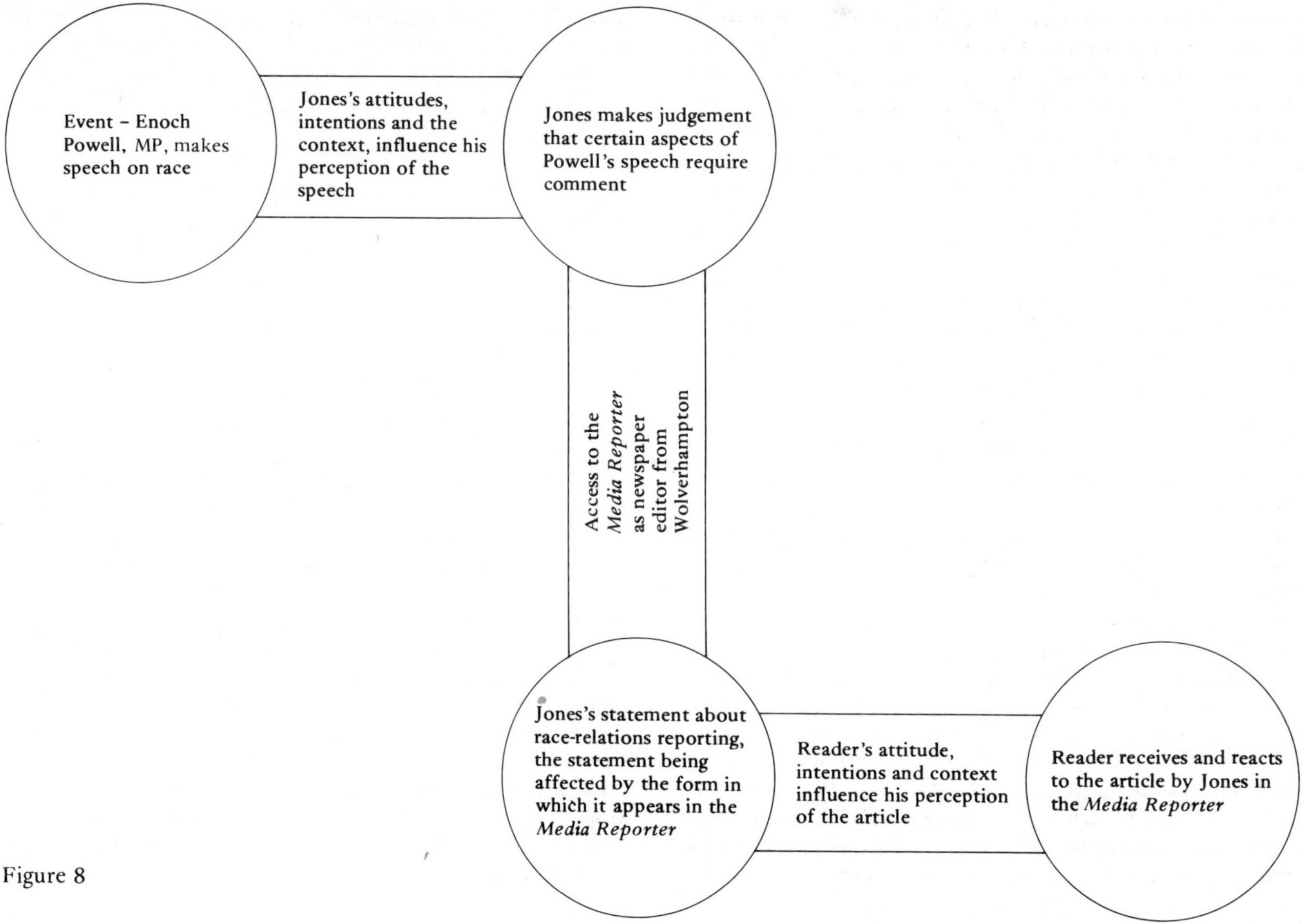

Event – Enoch Powell, MP, makes speech on race

Jones's attitudes, intentions and the context, influence his perception of the speech

Jones makes judgement that certain aspects of Powell's speech require comment

Access to the *Media Reporter* as newspaper editor from Wolverhampton

Jones's statement about race-relations reporting, the statement being affected by the form in which it appears in the *Media Reporter*

Reader's attitude, intentions and context influence his perception of the article

Reader receives and reacts to the article by Jones in the *Media Reporter*

Figure 8

M2 marks a transformation from SE into SE1. Again, the receiver of the message brings his own nature, intentions, set of needs and culture, to the message. The meaning that results will therefore possibly vary from receiver to receiver; and it is unlikely that the full potential in the message will be received without loss or gain.

A reader who has a hostile attitude to coloured immigrants, for example, will find meanings in the message different from those found by a reader with the opposite attitude. This model rightly implies that communication is much more complicated than Shannon and Weaver's early model suggests. Specifically, in this example, we might represent the process as in figure 8.

Gatekeeping

When Jones talks in his article of the influence of editors upon public opinion, he is talking of the power of *gatekeeping* in the mass media. The metaphor of a 'gatekeeper' derives from the image of an editor sitting in his office receiving news stories from a number of sources — the agencies, his reporters, the public, and so on. For some stories he 'opens the gate', or allows them on to the next stage of the process. For others he 'closes the gate' and they end up in his waste-paper basket. Gatekeeping studies investigate which stories are allowed through and which are rejected at each stage of the process, and they can shed a lot of light on the values and criteria that underlie each act of selection.

So gatekeepers determine which message is transmitted, and how it will be transmitted — they work in the vertical dimension of Gerbner's model. But gatekeeping is not confined to the mass media; it occurs in interpersonal and medio communication as well. Schramm (1960) points out:

At every point along the chain, someone has the right to say whether the message shall be received and retransmitted, and whether it shall be retransmitted in the same form or with changes . . . all along the chain are a series of gatekeepers, who have the right to open or close the gate to any message that comes along. (p. 170)

MacShane (1979), introducing the ways in which it is possible for members of the public to check and complain about any abuses of such power by 'gatekeepers', comments that 'journalists should be under constant pressure to be fair'.

Gerbner's model makes useful reference to the process of selection which takes place in the conveying of a message. This process is also evident in the practices of the mass media, which finally consist, after all, of numerous individuals aggregating selections for the production of a piece of communication for a mass audience.

Let's look at some of the important ways in which selection can occur in the mass media. Let's expand the notion of gatekeeping and consider which people in our society tend to have access to the mass media. Document 10 is an example from the 'quality' press. It is another editorial, this time from the *Sunday Times* (1 February 1981). The writer is arguing that one owner rather than another should have access to the newspaper which the writer works for. He is arguing that Rupert Murdoch, who wished to buy the newspaper, should be allowed to do so. (The Thomson Organization announced in 1980 that it wanted to sell Times Newspapers Ltd, since it could not see the group becoming profitable. By January 1981, Rupert Murdoch, the owner of the *Sun* and the *News of the World* in Britain, and of News International Ltd, had made a bid for Times Newspapers.)

DOCUMENT 10

Of course, the anxieties about concentration of proprietorial power are understandable. Yet the risk is not, as some of our readers seem to fear, of an invasion of page 3 of the *Sunday Times*. There is as little prospect of that as of *Sun* readers being invited to study five columns of the Law Report every morning. The risk is that the power of ownership could be abused, as it has so often been abused in Fleet Street, to impose a common political line. This is too substantial a question to be brushed aside because of the brinkmanship imposed by the Thomson timetable. The decisions made now will be a more-or-less permanent feature of our landscape.

The legitimate, though not conclusive, points against a Monopolies reference are three. Firstly, and most weakly, Britain enjoys, even with common ownership, more competition between national daily and regional newspapers than any other country. Secondly, there is a risk that a rejection of Mr Murdoch would jeopardise *The Times*. The

Sunday Times could stand on its own feet but *The Times* would be unlikely to avoid an interruption of publication. There are a number of things we do not like about being part of Times Newspapers, as we have made clear, but we would not want to expose *The Times* to risk, not least when Mr Murdoch's drive might revive it.

Thirdly, there are the editorial guarantees. Mr Murdoch might own four national newspapers, but Express Newspapers owns the *Daily Express*, the *Sunday Express*, the *Star* and half the *Evening Standard*; the IPC group owns the *Daily Mirror*, the *Sunday Mirror* and the *Sunday People*; Associated Newspapers owns the *Daily Mail* and eleven provincial newspapers; and Thomson, denuded of Times Newspapers, still owns 15 important provincial dailies — and none, even including Thomson, has such entrenched guarantees as are in prospect at Times Newspapers.

There is thus a very good case for the Murdoch proposal; but it is for the Minister to

apply the Monopolies law and for parliament to satisfy itself that the viable and unobjectionable alternatives have been properly considered and that the Murdoch guarantees are sound. The timetable for completion of the deal and the inevitability of confidentiality have created suspicion—and we would like a better beginning for Times Newspapers than a political row. We would especially like to stop making news ourselves.

The editorial contains references which need clarification. This is necessary either because the *context* of the article has now changed (and consequently the understanding that the audience is assumed to possess), or because a fuller explanation of the terms referred to has been omitted in this extract. We have reproduced here only that part of the editorial which seems relevant to our *purpose*: our discussion of the power of gatekeepers in the mass media. (We are the gatekeepers now!) 'Page 3' is a reference to the topless girls who appear daily on page 3 of the popular newspaper the *Sun*. 'A Monopolies reference' concerns the possibility that Murdoch's proposed acquisition of Times Newspapers would be investigated by the Monopolies Commission, a government-established body which is supposed to limit the concentration of industrial power into too few hands. (In fact the reference to the Commission was never made, on the grounds that the ensuing delay would inevitably mean closure or an interruption of publication; and that the guarantees of editorial independence given by Murdoch were sufficient to allay fears of the abuse of concentration of power in the newspaper industry. It is further interesting to note that the third paragraph of the editorial points out that it is not normal for most British newspapers to possess such guarantees of editorial independence from their proprietors.)

In an article in the *New Statesman* (30 January 1981) entitled 'Into the arms of Count Dracula', covering Murdoch's record in allowing his editors their independence, Bruce Page, editor of the *New Statesman* and formerly an investigative journalist with the *Sunday Times* itself, wrote:

DOCUMENT 11

LAST SATURDAY afternoon, the *Sunday Times* composing room exhibited the disciplined chaos which is normal when the paper is going to press. But there was a novel presence: the compact, energetic figure of Rupert Murdoch, eager rescuer of the troubled *Times* group, and loudly-advertised guarantor — potentially, anyway — of the editorial independence of its newspapers.

He cast a sharp, professional eye over the page-proofs as they came up for checking. One in particular excited his interest: it carried a long leading-article stating the *Sunday Times'* public attitude to the takeover. The leader was friendly in tone, and had a passage dealing with proposals for a Monopolies Commission inquiry — something violently opposed by Murdoch.

Cogent arguments against such an idea were cited. But, as it seemed to Murdoch, they could be more cogent still. He, as the text said, 'might own four national newspapers, but Express Newspapers owns the *Daily Express,* the *Sunday Express,* and half the *Evening Standard* . . .' The leader-writer had omitted the *Star,* another Express possession.

The boss of News International scribbled on his proof, and beckoned a *Sunday Times* executive. The passage (see illustration) appeared in the final edition in the form which Murdoch preferred. (An argument justifying further

Thirdly, and overwhelmingly, there are the editorial guarantees. Mr Murdoch might own four national newspapers, but Express Newspapers owns the Daily Express, the Sunday Express, and half the Evening Standard; the IPC group owns the Daily Mirror, the Sunday Mirror and the Sun.

Thirdly, there are the editorial guarantees. Mr Murdoch might own four national newspapers, but Express Newspapers owns the Daily Express, the Sunday Express, The Star and half the Evening Standard; the IPC group owns the Daily Mirror, the Sunday Mirror and the Sunday

The Sunday Times leader before (above) and after (below) Murdoch's interference

monopoly through existing monopoly is shoddy enough: it becomes more so when a sick paper like the *Star* is counted against a money-spinner like the *Sun*.)

Thus, the *Sunday Times* leader which celebrated Rupert Murdoch's readiness to avoid interfering with *Sunday Times* leaders was one which Murdoch himself had checked, altered and approved. And it did not express in any serious way the doubts which many of the paper's journalists feel about the propriety, and necessity, of the News International take-over. (*The Times'* leader on Murdoch was also checked by Murdoch.)

For non-journalists, it's worth spelling-out that the composing-room is the critical area in a newspaper office. The idea of outsiders entering and checking-over references to their business deals is wholly unheard-of. And most proprietors — however slight their commitment to editorial independence — eschew personal interference in the process which occurs when the newspapers they own are converting judgments into type. Mr Murdoch, however, is something else again: he will do it to a newspaper even before he owns it. And it's against this background that Mr John Biffen, the Trade Secretary, should read News International's 'guarantees' about the future liberties of *The Times* and *Sunday Times*.

In terms of Gerbner's model, the event to which Page refers took place when 'the boss of News International scribbled on his proof, and beckoned a *Sunday Times* executive'.

In his reply to Page's article (in the *New Statesman*, 6 February 1981), Harold Evans (who was later briefly editor of *The Times* before resigning over Murdoch's alleged interference) did not deny that this event occurred, but saw things differently.

DOCUMENT 12

On the stone

From Harold Evans, editor, Sunday Times

Before it passes into mythology I must correct the false impression you gave in your story about Rupert Murdoch and the *Sunday Times* editorial (*NS* 30 January). You state a true fact, then add to it an interpretation and conclude with a speculation by which time you are about 1000 miles from the starting point. The correct facts are as follows.

Mr Murdoch was visiting the *Sunday Times* composing room, as management and owners have done in the past. He was shown by somebody my editorial page and I suppose it would take a super human being not to want to read it. He noticed that the leader had omitted the *Star* among the list of Express newspapers and drew this to the attention of somebody. A helpful gesture, you might say. In any event, he did not ask for it to be corrected, he did not 'approve' the editorial or pass any judgment at all on it. Because of the risk of mis-perception, I have discussed the incident with Mr Murdoch and nothing like it will occur again. Of that I am satisfied.

You went to great trouble to show a first and final edition to demonstrate that we had corrected a factual omission. If you had been fair you might have let your readers share the knowledge that the first and final editions of the editorial differed — in ways which undermined the hypothesis you laboured to create.

Evans argues here that distortion has taken place through Page's 'perceptual dimension' — as the process has developed from E to E1 in Gerbner's model. He claims, therefore, that Page's statement about the event, SE, is further distorted, since he fails to include in his article the information that the 'first and final editions of the editorial differed'. Consequently, argues Evans (though without quoting from the original editorial further to prove his point), the statement as perceived by the reader, SE1, will also fail to be a 'correct' fact about an event which all agree took place that Saturday afternoon.

It is interesting to note that in terms of ideology Page and Evans do not disagree: both share the view, apparently, that the gatekeepers should be the people who write newspaper articles and editorials, that is the journalists and editors, not the owners, such as Murdoch. An ideological difference between them would exist if, for example, Page maintained that newspapers should not operate with the editor having such special influence, but that some collective expression of editorial opinion should be allowed to develop.

Evidently, at a national level, access to the mass media is not equal, since there were fewer than half-a-dozen groups able to make realistic offers to take over these newspapers when this section of the 'free press' became available. Thus the activities of gatekeepers (editors, sub-editors, journalists, etc.) appear to be influenced by the outlook and philosophy of the wealthy people (such as Rupert Murdoch) who control the large newspaper corporations. The difficulties encountered by journalists who try to resist such pressures are well exemplified by the case of the *Camden Journal*, a local newspaper in North London.

On 19 December 1980, the closure of the *Camden Journal* was announced and its nine journalists were sacked. The journalists claim that neither the readers nor the journalists were asked for their views before the closure was announced. Since talks about the closure with the NUJ were refused by the management, and since the journalists were given only a few days to decide whether they could take over the title themselves, the NUJ called an official strike affecting other papers in the group, arguing that the paper should continue, possibly with some negotiated early retirements or voluntary redundancies from the staff. They put their arguments against closure thus:

DOCUMENT 13

Putting the record straight

Why do the owners of the Journal want to close it down?

They say it was making a loss. But they have repeatedly failed to produce any real figures backing up their case.

They say it did not attract advertising. Again, they have not produced a single figure to substantiate this.

Moreover, we have discovered in the past few weeks that the Journal did not seem interested in getting ads in Camden! Time and again, traders have told us, 'The Journal never asked us to advertise.'

They say that although circulation rose from 2000 in the early seventies to 6500 two years ago, it has remained static ever since.

What they do NOT say is that unlike the great majority of newspapers — including our competitors in Camden—the Journal have not distributed the paper on a 'sale or return' basis.

We have also discovered that TWO YEARS AGO the management stopped 'topping up' initial sales at newsagents on Friday by distributing extra copies. This is normal practice with our competitors.

They say they have financial problems. Then why has the company, which owns a string of daily papers and weeklies in the Midlands, been buying up more?

Two years ago they bought papers in West Wales. Recently they bought a print works at Great Yarmouth, publishing lucrative government documents.

SO WHAT'S THE REAL REASON FOR THE CLOSURE?

We say it's because management did not like the editorial policies of the paper — too independent and anti-establishment for their liking — and because many of the staff are loyal members of the NUJ, including assistant editor Howard Hannah, chairman of the union's North London Branch, and editor, Eric Gordon, chairman of the London Council of the NUJ, and a negotiator in last year's London Weighting dispute.

The journalists also responded, helped by sympathetic members of the local community, by producing their own paper, *Save The Journal*, at first four pages, later eight. In the third issue Chris Goodall, assistant editor on another newspaper in the North London News Ltd group, the *Islington Gazette*, wrote:

DOCUMENT 14

A pressing need for real freedom

by Chris Goodall,
Islington Gazette Assistant Editor

'NECESSITY is the plea for every infringement of freedom. It is the argument of tyrants; it is the creed of slaves.'

If the words are familiar, it is because they have been around for a long time.

They were first used by William Pitt during a Parliamentary skirmish in 1788.

I recalled them when I first heard of the actions of the directors of North London News Ltd in proposing the closure of the *Camden Journal*.

They claim that economic necessity is forcing them to deprive the people of Camden of the freedom to read a lively local paper that cares passionately about the borough it serves.

I don't suppose they would put it quite like that. I expect thet would regard the use of words like 'freedom' as emotive. After all, press freedom usually has a very different meaning in the vocabulary of newspaper owners — particularly those in Fleet Street.

It is trotted out on special occasions when they feel threatened:
— WHEN printers object to setting in type stories villifying striking trade unionists.
— WHEN minority groups demand space to put their case.
— WHEN civil-rights campaigners suggest that it is wrong to subject an accused man to trial by newspaper.

I believe that press freedom has a much wider meaning.

It means ensuring access to newspaper columns for people who have a view but no voice.

It means more space for the issues that affect people's lives — bad housing, poor schools — and less for page 3 'tits and bums'.

Above all it means fighting to ensure that papers like the *Camden Journal* are not killed off solely because they do not measure up to an accountant's idea of an acceptable profit margin.

Gatekeeping: a model

The process of gatekeeping in the mass media has been theoretically presented by Westley and MacLean (1957) (figure 9).

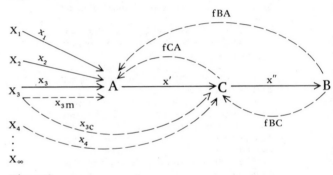

Figure 9

Note The messages C transmits to B (x″) represent his selections from both messages to him from A's (x′) and C's selections and abstractions from Xs in his own sensory field (X_{3C}, X_4), which may or may not be Xs in A's field. Feedback not only moves from B to A (fBA) and from B to C (fBC) but also from C to A (fCA).

Let's consider the model in terms of the article we have just read. In this instance:

A — Goodall, the journalist, the assistant editor, the would-be communicator or 'advocate'.

B — the reader of the article in *Save the Journal*, the audience.

C — the gatekeepers (editor and sub-editors) of *Save the Journal*, the people who control this medium.

X — any event or object (e.g. the closure of the *Camden Journal*, William Pitt's 1788 statement, the argument about 'press freedom') which A, B or C are aware of.

F — feedback, communication back from B to the original advocate of the message (A).

The messages which the article by Goodall (A) transmits to the reader (B) include:

1. Selections of what is said by A (i.e. C may have cut the article down due to lack of space).
2. Selections from events in B's own sensory field (X3c, X4), which may or may not be events in A's field (e.g. C thinks up the headline to the article, it was not included by Goodall in the original article — it becomes, as the result of C's intervention as sub-editor, part of the total message.

Feedback moves:

1. From B to A (fBA), e.g. a letter from a reader to the editor of *Save the Journal* commenting on the article by Goodall.
2. From B to C (fBC), e.g. a letter from a reader direct to Goodall at the *Islington Gazette*.
3. From C to A (fCA), e.g. a memo from the editor of *Save the Journal* to Goodall saying how much his article was appreciated by his staff and requesting another article for the next issue.

In the case above, B, the readership of *Save the Journal*, can be numbered in thousands, C in tens (the editor and sub-editors), and A is a single individual.

In the typical mass-communication situation, however, there will be many more As (working, for example, for a newspaper the size of the *Sunday Times*) transmitting messages through a large number of Cs to a mass readership to be numbered in hundreds of thousands.

Westley and MacLean's model suggests that today B is very much at the mercy of C, who plays a dominant role in communication with A. Now while this is certainly true (as the *Sunday Times* editorial on mergers of newspapers indicates), it is not realistic to present B as totally dependent on the mass media, with no access to the events of the real world. We do check (though maybe not often enough) the stories put out by the media with reference to the real world. To come back to our earlier example, Enoch Powell's argument that race relations in Britain are steadily worsening might be checked by anyone with some experience of living in an area inhabited by people of differing ethnic origins.

Westley and MacLean suggest that their model may be applied to types of communication other than mass, and you should consider the applicability of their examples to other case-study material. They suggest that B can be:

1. A person: e.g. a housewife who is too busy to rush around and observe the neighbourhood. C is the neighbourhood gossip who observes, selects and encodes a limited portion of all possible messages, supplying the needs of B.
2. A primary group: e.g. a relatively isolated frontier colony which posts sentinels (Cs) to observe and report the

condition of the environment by means of a special code such as a rifle shot. Bs would also greet eagerly the arrival of another kind of C, the rider who returns to the colony bearing important information.

3. A social system: e.g. a national state requires and maintains an elaborate network of Cs performing such special information functions as that of the diplomatic service.

ASSIGNMENT J

1. Apply the Gerbner/Fiske model to the editorial in *Save the Journal*.
2. Apply the Westley and MacLean model to the editorial in the *Sunday Times*.
3. Compare the usefulness of the two models in throwing light on the process that has occurred in the writing and production of these two editorials.

CASE STUDIES:
THINKING ABOUT PRACTICE

4

The material included in this chapter is intended to develop more communication skills, raise further theoretical issues, and to get you thoroughly used to thinking in depth about the processes of communication in which you are involved. The content of the case studies follows some of the themes introduced already, with particular emphasis upon persuasive communication. We shall be looking in detail at some examples of how professional communicators attempt to influence their audiences.

Persuasive communication

We should first ask ourselves some basic questions about the nature of persuasive communication itself. As an example, let us consider the art of writing rhetoric. How can we learn to use written verbal symbols to persuade others to our point of view? Are models and rules useful in learning the practice? Is imitating the 'best' examples the way to learn the art?

The book from which I have taken the following example itself presents certain problems of classification. What type of communication is it? Robert M. Pirsig's *Zen and the Art of Motorcycle Maintenance* (1976) is avowedly fiction and is normally to be found on the fiction shelf of a bookshop. By context, then, most browsers and experts in the book trade take this to be a novel; yet it is sub-titled: 'An inquiry into values'. The extract we shall take from this book is intended to help you reflect on the value of the models of communication to which you have just been introduced. The central character, Phaedrus, is himself dealing with the problems posed by different types of writing, and authorial intention and method. He is here thinking about his past experiences of trying to teach rhetoric to students in English classes at the University of Montana, Bozeman, USA. He refers to the university as the 'Church of Reason' because he believes that everything that happens there should be based on rationality. 'Rhetoric' is defined by the *Concise Oxford English Dictionary* as 'the art of persuasive or impressive speaking or writing; language designed to persuade or impress' (the technique used, for example, by the editor in writing his newspaper editorial).

DOCUMENT 15

He *was* thinking hard: the crushing teaching load was bad enough, but what for him was far worse was that he understood in his precise analytic way that the subject he was teaching was undoubtedly the most unprecise, unanalytic, amorphous area in the entire Church of Reason. That's why he was thinking so hard. To a methodical, laboratory-trained mind, rhetoric is just completely hopeless. It's like a huge Sargasso Sea of stagnated logic.

What you're supposed to do in most freshman-rhetoric courses is to read a little essay or short story, discuss how the writer has done certain little things to achieve certain little effects, and then have the students write an imitative little essay or short story to see if they can do the same little things. He tried this over and over again but it never jelled. The students seldom achieved anything, as a result of this calculated mimicry, that was remotely close to the models he'd given them. More often their writing got worse. It seemed as though every rule he honestly tried to discover with them and learn with them was so full of exceptions and contradictions and qualifications and confusions that he wished he'd never come across the rule in the first place.

A student would always ask how the rule would apply in a certain special circumstance. Phaedrus would then have the choice of trying to fake through a made-up explanation of how it worked, or follow the selfless route and say what he really thought. And what he really thought was that the rule was *pasted on* to the writing after the writing was all done. It was *post hoc*, after the fact, instead of prior to the fact. And he became convinced that all the writers the students were supposed to mimic wrote without rules, putting down whatever sounded right, then going back to see if it still sounded right and changing it if it didn't. There were some who apparently wrote with calculating premeditation because that's the way their product looked. But that seemed to him to be a very poor way to look. It had a certain syrup, as Gertrude Stein once said, but it didn't pour. But how're you to teach something that isn't premeditated? It was a seemingly impossible requirement. He just took the text and commented on it in an unpremeditated way and hoped the students would get something from that. It wasn't satisfactory. (pp. 170–1)

Learning by imitation?

Let's try to analyse the reasons for the problems that Phaedrus and the students are facing here, since this will deepen our understanding of the relationship between persuasive writing and audiences. Phaedrus *feels* that the best persuasive writers have written by instinct first and then only changed what did not seem to them to be right. They have not written to formulae or to models. But Phaedrus is supposed, according to traditional teaching methods in rhetoric, to get his students to study these great writers, extract the rules or model from their writing, and then, using the model, imitate them. Invariably, however, Phaedrus finds that this method is unsuccessful. Premeditated writing seems to be bad writing.

The problem arises in this form partly because of the absence of a specific audience at whom the pieces of persuasive writing are aimed. In the case of essays or short stories, the reader at whom the writing is aimed may not be specified very clearly at all in the writer's mind. S/he will not need to stop and calculate, to premeditate, because s/he will not have that precise an aim; or at least s/he will not have a set of rules or a model *separate* from the writing. S/he will look at it when complete, and consider whether or not it *feels* right. If it doesn't, s/he will adjust it. The problem arises for the students then, because you are asking them to learn a process by performing the task in a manner that the original performer ignored.

When you write critical essays on English literature texts you are not likely to face the same problems; in this case you are not supposed to be writing primarily from *feeling*, as you might be if you were writing a poem. Certainly the aim of your essay is to *persuade* the person who marks it that your feelings and views about the text have substance — but there is an established form, rules and model that you can use. You know that you must use quotations from the text and comment on the text in detail. You must introduce your subject, give examples and evidence for your arguments, and write a concluding paragraph. The structure is there, and the audience, the examiner, is there too, even if you don't know very much about him or her. The problem for Phaedrus's students when they struggle with their short stories is that there are simply so many variables that reason cannot begin to operate effectively. There are no concrete aids as far as audience and structure are concerned. All they have is a set of rules, a model, which they try to apply to *feelings*. And the two forces work in separate directions.

The range of writing required in most English literature courses in this country is still extremely limited. Since the range of writing required of communication studies students doing case-study work is much greater, the student is given more detail about the final result required. The more the requirements are specified, the more testable the result: does the writing achieve the desired result on the specified audience? We are not, normally, left without guidance as Phaedrus is. He simply commented on the writing 'in an unpremeditated way and hoped the students would get something from that'. This echoes the problem commented on by Charles Schermerhorn Schuyler, a nineteenth-century writer in Gore Vidal's novel, *1876* (1976): 'Well, the writer is not unlike the explorer. We, too, are searching for lost cities, rare tigers, the sentence never before written.'

But whatever type of writing we are considering, and

however specific the aims and audience, the following terms should be found useful:

Dialect Specialized selections of words and forms of expression which are distinctive of geographical or social groups.

Register A dialect associated with a particular function, occupation or profession (e.g. journalism, science, religion).

Syntax The combination of words into significant patterns (e.g. sentences).

Semantics The association of words and word patterns with 'meaning'.

Collocation The tendency of words to occur in regular association (e.g. 'happy' with 'event'; 'satisfaction' with 'customers').

Style The possibility of variations on the normal forms of language for special purposes or emphasis, persuasion, emotional effect, etc.

ASSIGNMENT K (Document 15)

1. Discuss the reasons for the relative failure of Phaedrus's principles for rhetoric teaching.
2. Define and discuss the essential differences between the audiences for, and the intentions behind, the following types of writing in Britain today:

   (a) a poem,
   (b) a short story,
   (c) a critical essay on a set novel in an English literature course.

Building a structure

The extract from *Zen and the Art of Motorcycle Maintenance* above is intended to stimulate reflection on the process taking place within *you* as as communicator.

Our next case study attempts to demonstrate how it is possible to draw up a conceptual scheme by which you can analyse material. What is needed is something on paper which is the referent for the concept. We are going to attempt something in the nature of a practical criticism, the fundamental activity of English literature studies. Our practical criticism should serve as a model indicating how suitable case-study materials can be approached. The structure for analysis grows out of the material focused upon. The detail of the stucture is not of crucial importance. What is important is that you always insist on *developing a structure* whenever you confront material. For the structure is at the interface between the material itself (the data of the real world) and your understanding of communication.

The data from the real world which we shall consider consists of aspects of the Buzby advertising campaign mounted on behalf of Post Office Telecommunications in the late 1970s. I shall refer to the following material — the four items in Document 16 — as the 'Buzby' case study.

DOCUMENT 16

PROMOTING THE TELEPHONE FOR THE FUTURE.

THE BACKGROUND.
Two tariff increases were introduced in 1975, the larger one in October. These increases were necessary in order to maintain our financial viability in a period of rapid cost inflation, but naturally public concern was aroused and management felt that our customers would think the telephone service more expensive than in fact it is.

Two National TV campaigns and one press campaign were run during the year from April 1st 1975, emphasising the continuing good value of long distance, direct-dialled Cheap Rate calls.

Market research has shown that public awareness of the good value of a 3-minute long distance, direct-dialled call has been significantly improved as a result of this advertising campaign.

PLANNING FOR THE FUTURE—THE PROBLEM.
Whilst these recent efforts have proved successful in improving public awareness, it has become clear to management that the telephone service's public image needs urgent attention, particularly during a period of return to profitability.

The advantages of owning a telephone are clear. But it would be wrong to ignore the real problems that exist for the phone service in the public's mind.

These are:
a) the telephone service, as part of the Post Office, is seen to be too large, sometimes inefficient, and often too expensive;
b) consequently, the service is regarded to some extent as unsympathetic, and possibly soulless.

Although these factors may appear a little extreme, they do represent an important segment of customer opinion.

THE PROMOTIONAL CHALLENGE.
Management recognises that the challenge for the future is to continue to promote the benefits of the telephone service, as we have done in the past, but to do so in a style which establishes a new and more friendly identity for the telephone.

THE PHONE SERVICE GETS A NEW PERSONALITY.
Our advertising agency has developed a cartoon character—a small, cheerful bird who naturally enough lives much of his life on a telephone wire.

"Hello"

WHY A CARTOON CHARACTER?

He is a friendly character who can speak in TV commercials for the telephone service as well as appear on posters or press advertisements designed for the residential market. He can talk to the public more sympathetically and convey a greater variety of information more acceptably than a real person could. As a drawn figure, he should increasingly act as a strong but friendly symbol of the telephone service.

HOW WILL HE WORK FOR US?

The bird will fly into people's homes all over the country for the first time in a major TV campaign starting at the end of May. In the opening commercial, as you can see from the stills, he will be reminding people how nice it is to give friends and relatives a call, and that it is still, in the Cheap Rate period, very good value for money.

Subsequently, he will appear on very large poster sites throughout the country during the summer, reminding people to make a phone call either in the evenings or at the weekends.

After Christmas, he will be back on television in new commercials. The total spread of advertising during the year, is shown in the plan below:

	MAY JUNE JULY AUG SEPT OCT NOV DEC JAN FEB
TV NATIONALLY	
POSTERS NATIONALLY	MAY JUNE JULY AUG SEPT OCT NOV DEC JAN FEB

Bird: 'Hey, listen to this.'
Voices on the Phone: 'Happy Birthday dear Grandma. Happy Birthday to you.'
Bird: 'Aaaaah, isn't that lovely. You know, making someone happy on the phone is so easy.'

And it really isn't expensive. In fact, it's quite cheap. Get it? Cheap-cheep. Oh well please yourselves.

Anyway, if you've got a phone and you dial direct, a full 3-minute Cheap Rate chat will cost you less than 10p. And that's the long distance price. Local calls are even cheaper.

So why not make someone happy this evening. And if they ask why you're phoning, tell them a little bird told you.'

Make someone happy with a Cheap Rate phone call.

Coinbox calls are charged at a higher rate.

EXTRACTS FROM THE 2 TELEVISION COMMERCIALS.

TESTING THE ADVERTISING.

A test is being planned in which the Granada TV area will have heavier-than-average advertising, whilst the Border TV area will carry no advertising. By assessing the difference in extra business generated in the test region, we hope to establish the right level of advertising needed to increase business nationally.

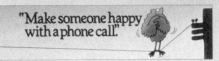

THE FUTURE.

Initial consumer research has shown that the cartoon bird is regarded as a very acceptable symbol for the telephone service.

People believe that he is a friendly and attractive character. Naturally, we will be controlling his development very carefully, but we are hopeful that he will prove to be a 'real winner' with our customers.

With the ultimate objective of substituting a warm and friendly image of our business for the present faceless and apparently non-caring one, his future is almost limitless. He can appear on all sorts of telephone service literature for the residential market; after his TV launch he will be available in photographic form for use by all regions for public and press relations as well as local promotions. His attractive personality should add impact, interest and warmth to all our promotional efforts to help present the telephone service as a more sympathetic organisation.

The bird with his foreign friends.

Post Office Telecommunications

NATIONAL INLAND CALL STIMULATION CAMPAIGN.

1977-78.

BACKGROUND.

The stimulation of inland calls needs sustained publicity.

Buzby will therefore continue the job which he began successfully last year, but with one change: the emphasis is switched from Cheap Rate to calling generally.

Research provided some very high recall figures and supported the case for continuity.

THE CAMPAIGN.

There will be an extra phase of TV and more extended use of posters, including boundary boards at important cricket matches throughout the season.

The following pages outline...

TELEVISION.

Stills from the 4 new commercials:

MAX BYGRAVES
Buzby attempts an impersonation of "Max Bygraves" and sings—"You need wings"
"Make someone happy with a phone call"

LAUGHING BUZBY
Buzby receives a telephone call—and obviously is highly amused by the speaker—as all he can do is laugh and laugh.
"Make someone happy with a phone call"

BUZBY'S MOTHER
Buzby calls up his mum and wishes her a happy birthday—and casually informs her that she is also appearing on TV!
"Make someone happy with a phone call"

BIRD BRAIN OF BRITAIN
Buzby is appearing on a quiz show—and is doing rather badly—however when asked 'How much does a cheap rate 3 minute long distance phone call cost' he answers correctly and is made 'Bird Brain of Britain'.
"Make someone happy with a phone call"

POSTERS.

"Make someone happy with a phone call."

National posters (10' x 20') One of two versions.

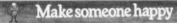

Make someone happy

Cricket sites

"Make someone happy with a phone call"

Van sides

THE ADVERTISING PLAN.												
	1977									1978		
	APR	MAY	JUN	JUL	AUG	SEP	OCT	NOV	DEC	JAN	FEB	MAR
TELEVISION		▬▬									▬	
POSTERS				▬▬▬▬▬▬▬								
CRICKET SITES	▬▬▬▬▬											

TELEVISION.

The national campaign will comprise 4 different 30 second commercials. A total of 200 spots will be seen.

Over 90% of all adults will, on average, have the opportunity to see the commercials 13 times.

POSTERS.

Between July and November, there will be two phases of national roadside advertising using 10' x 20' posters, positioning will depend on the sites available. In London, Underground and BR main line termini sites will be used. An animated sign in Piccadilly Circus is also planned.

CRICKET GROUNDS.

Buzby will be appearing at five major cricket grounds this season. These sites will be viewed by spectators and television viewers alike.

The grounds are: Lords, Trent Bridge, Headingly, Oval, Old Trafford, plus 10 major county sites around England.

VAN SIDES.

The existing successful van side poster design will continue in use.

BUZBY MERCHANDISING.

This is beginning with the commercial exploitation of T-shirts, and should extend to the toy market by Christmas.

STIMULATING LOCAL CALLS IN LONDON.1977-78.

BACKGROUND

The London Telecommunications Region is the largest in the country, accounting for nearly one third of all phone connections. Local calls represent very good value for money—giving, as they do, access over a wide area to five million telephones.

Whilst phone usage has been increasing in recent years, we have not specifically promoted local calls, for which we believe there is much scope for potential growth.

With this in mind, it has been decided to launch a heavy-weight advertising and publicity campaign in the London region in June to encourage local calls.

THE ADVERTISING PLAN

Overleaf, details are given of the plan. Both commercial advertising media and Post Office publicity media will be utilised, generating, it is hoped, a strong, successful campaign.

Naturally, Buzby will be leading the effort, both on television and on posters, bus-sides and other print material.

TELEVISION ADVERTISING AND POSTERS

1st Commercial

'Nelson' – Buzby is perched on Nelson's column viewing London through a telescope. The telephone rings and Buzby answers it however the caller wishes to speak to Nelson in person! "Make someone happy with a local call"

2nd Commercial

'Eros' – Buzby is seen on Eros playing with a bow and arrow – accidentally he fires an arrow and blames Eros! – however Eros is himself answering a phone call. "Make someone happy with a local call"

London Underground, and British Rail Posters

A local call brings people together.

A local call goes a long way.

London Bus-Sides

POST OFFICE MEDIA

Van Sides

Phone Kiosk Posters

Bill Envelope Leaflet *(front)*   *(inside)*

THE ADVERTISING PLAN

TELEVISION
June 11th-30th. Over 90% of adults will see a commercial, on average, over 13 times. 80 spots will be broadcast in this period.

L.T. BUS SIDES
About 1000 of London's buses will carry the impressive poster throughout June and will be seen by virtually everybody who lives or works in the London Region.

L.T. UNDERGROUND AND B.R. STATIONS
4-sheet posters will appear at tube stations and on display panels at British Rail's London Termini. People who travel around London everyday will see the "Local Call" message prominently displayed.

POST OFFICE MEDIA
Our own vans and many phone kiosks will carry posters reflecting the local message, whilst customers in LTR will receive a leaflet in their bill envelope as a follow-up to the June campaign.

How Buzby was hatched
R M Stanley

EIGHTEEN months ago Buzby was not even conceived let alone hatched. Today he is to be seen all over Britain on television screens, on poster sites, on the London Underground and buses, on the Post Office's own huge fleet of vehicles, and at exhibitions. His jaunty figure is also familiar at County cricket grounds, on millions of Post Office leaflets, and he will shortly be appearing on telephone bill envelopes.

But that is not all. He is illuminated in Piccadilly Circus, and he appears in advertisements in national, provincial and local newspapers and magazines. He is already a T-shirt favourite and by Christmas there will be a range of Buzby toys and games. And last, but not least, Telephone Areas all over the country have invented their own ways of adapting him for use in their own local promotional material.

A meteoric rise indeed. But who is Buzby, why was he born and what objectives has he been designed to fulfil? It was towards the end of 1975, following two tariff increases in a short time that public concern was aroused and there was strong evidence that people thought the telephone service was much more expensive than, in fact, it was.

Research showed that the actual cost of a cheap rate trunk call was unacceptably low.

Indeed, many people thought it was up to six times as much as it really was. There was clearly a need to stimulate more calls and particularly to publicise the low cost of trunk calls made during cheap rate periods.

A start was therefore made early in 1976 with a national television campaign which showed a 10p coin rolling across the screen and telling people how far 10p could get them even in days of rising prices. Before-and-after surveys showed a steep rise in awareness during the period of the campaign, but there was a marked fall-off soon after the campaign finished.

When planning the campaign strategy for the year from April 1976 it was, therefore, vital to get as much continuity as possible, but it was equally important to achieve as much memorability and goodwill from the proposed advertising as possible. The question was how best to vest the advertising with an image that would be warm and friendly but, above all, memorable.

Since the objective was to humanise and personalise the Post Office image there were really two choices. A live personality could be used as presenter or a cartoon could be devised to fit the bill as the co-ordinating symbol for publicity.

The drawbacks of using a person as presenter were obvious. Whoever was selected would not be everybody's choice, and such advertising – particularly on television – could draw attention to the person and his image, often at the expense of the advertising mes-

sage. Also there is the fact that any one person is vulnerable to human factors such as illness or other commitments.

There is the point, too, that it would be very difficult to select any personality who would appeal to both business and residential markets. This is borne out by the fact that no business, industry or corporation which advertises nationally has, over the past 20 years, used a live personality to present its case except in very minor campaigns.

The case for cartoon-type characters is altogether stronger. This is why the gas industry used Mr Therm, why Tate and Lyle use Mr Cube and why Shell has animated its own Shell symbol. The Telecommunications Business is very fortunate in the wide availability of outlets available for publicity purposes for, in addition to all forms of paid media advertising, it has the largest transport fleet in the country and it produces continuously, vast quantities of literature for distribution to its customers. About 50 million account envelopes reach the public in any one year, for instance.

There is wide evidence that cartoon characters appeal to most people regardless of class or age group. This is why Mickey Mouse is now celebrating a jubilee, why the Wombles sell over £16 million worth of toys a year, and why Robertson's can still use the golliwog for their products. It was with this knowledge that Buzby was conceived and soon afterwards made his television debut.

Three commercials were used during 1976 showing Buzby in various situa-

...tions on the wires near his telephone post. In one he was listening, entranced, to children wishing their grandma a happy birthday, in another he was speaking affectionately, supposedly to his girl friend, only to find to his embarrassment that it was his mother, and finally he did a daring high-wire act by riding a 10p coin across the line and marvelling at the cheapness of a call.

The first television campaign ran between May and July and the second was at the end of the year running into the current year.

Between these campaigns there was a national poster campaign all over the country using more than 1,000 of the very large 48-sheet sites. Two separate posters were used, one for daylight and one for the evening, with Buzby wondering whom he should ring to make happy.

In the meantime, the Post Office Telecommunications vehicles were using back-up posters on an ever increasing scale and this helped considerably to ensure that Buzby was kept permanently and prominently in the public's eye.

Towards the end of 1976 the original slogan "Make someone happy with a cheap rate phone call" was changed to accord with the policy of emphasising value once the price has been sufficiently established. It then became "Make someone happy with a phone call". Currently as Buzby is becoming clearly identified with telephone calls, the slogan is being further shortened to simply "Make someone happy".

So what has Buzby achieved? Results have been spectacular on the internal front, where he has clearly filled the need of staff all over the country for a warm visual identification of the business for which they work. Enthusiasm in Areas to use him for every conceivable purpose has been unbounded.

As far as marketing objectives are concerned it is difficult to measure achievement precisely. Advertising is only one of many things which can influence people in the use they make of their telephones, and simply because there was a substantial increase in cheap rate trunk calls does not necessarily mean that it was due to the advertising campaign. The only reliable method of measuring the success of advertising is by measuring the awareness of the public to the message conveyed through the advertising.

On this basis the Buzby campaigns have met all the objectives set for them. A more precise test in which Granada TV had heavier than average advertising, while Border TV carried no advertising at all, is now being assessed to see whether it can produce any additional information on what the campaign has so far achieved.

The programme for the 12 months from April this year is more heavily on television advertising than 1976, and four new commercials have been produced to emphasise the happiness and value theme. In one, Buzby imitates showbusiness star Max Bygraves, in another he shows delirious happiness by his laughter during a phone call, in a third he speaks to his mother with Irene Handl lending her voice, and finally he is made "bird brain of Britain" by giving the correct answer to the cost of a cheap rate call after doing rather badly on simpler questions.

There will again be a national poster campaign from July until the end of November, and during the summer large posters will be on all the cricket grounds where Test Matches are being played and also on most County grounds. A supply of posters for Telecommunications vans will continue throughout the year and it is hoped that by Christmas the many toys and novelties featuring Buzby, now being developed, will be in the shops and on sale to the public.

Clearly Buzby has won an affectionate place in the hearts of Post Office staff and there is every reason to suppose that he will become a firm favourite with the public. His usefulness is constantly being extended and it seems he will be spreading his wings and his message for a long time to come.

Mr R. M. Stanley is head of Publicity Division at Telecommunications Headquarters and was responsible, in collaboration with the advertising agency, for devising the Buzby character.

PO Telecommunications Journal Summer 1977

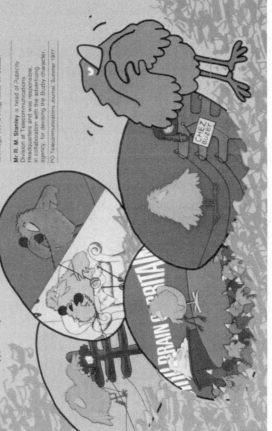

Approaching the material

How are we to approach this material? The suggestions made here should serve as a model which can be used to approach other material. First we need to *classify* the material, using brief notes to describe its essential content and purpose:

(a) *'Promoting the telephone for the future'* A document setting out the need for a national campaign, introducing Buzby, the motif in the material, and explaining how Buzby is to be used. This document seems to be aimed at people employed by the Post Office and involved in the campaign.

(b) *'National inland call stimulation campaign'* A document describing how the use of the telephone is to be stimulated generally and giving examples of sites for advertising, and possible content of advertising. Audience for document: as for (a), above.

(c) *'Stimulating local calls in London'* A document emphasizing the importance of London to the Post Office, giving examples of sites for advertising and possible content of advertising in London. Audience for document: as for (a) above.

(d) *'How Buzby was hatched'* An article by the Head of Publicity Division at Telecommunications headquarters. Audience for document: readers of the journal published for practitioners in advertising and publicity.

When making notes you should always consider the purpose for making them *before* you start. Do you expect the notes you are making to serve as the basis for a total recall of the original text? Are they intended to serve as a physical substitute for the original? Are they intended primarily to help you assimilate the original material? Will anybody other than you be making use of them?

Considering these questions should help you to decide upon the nature and length of the notes you will make. You should remember, also, that in a limited number of cases extensive note taking can actually inhibit understanding. Sansom (1972), writing of the manner in which he composes short stories, comments that 'it is also important for me that these notes are no more than a telegraphic message. Notes can be dangerous. If they are written out in full, they can too easily also fulfil the function of writing the idea out of oneself.'

This process of note making is recommended as a device for initially clarifying the distinctions between the subject matter and audience for each of the various documents. We lack the space here to analyse each of the documents in depth. We shall concentrate instead on the one which raises the most theoretical issues about communication: 'How Buzby was hatched.'

First we should notice the *presentation* of the material. What are the communicators (writer, artist, editor) trying to achieve by using the chosen layout? The pictures are intended as a familiar and humorous sign to attract readers of the journal. We notice that the pictures and border completely enclose the text, and that the total printed content completely fill two sides of A4 paper, without any significant space left. The appearance of the article is therefore compact and dense. A small typeface has been chosen and the page has been divided into three columns to include as many words as possible. Rather than divide the text up with cross headings (as in many newspaper layouts) the text has here been surrounded with related artwork.

Next we should apply the following modified version of Lasswell's model to the material before us:

1. Who?
2. Is attempting to attract whom?
3. Using which devices?
4. To receive which message?
5. In which context?
6. For what purpose?
7. And with what effect?

Stating results of analysis

At this stage we should note that we have no data with which to attempt an answer to 7. To help you become familiar with any such case-study material, you should attempt to answer each of the above questions in as much detail as possible. As an example we shall consider here how you might approach that part of (d) above which deals with the *written* message.

It is useful to divide the text into paragraphs and ask of each: 'What is going on here? What is the writer trying to communicate here?' Our results might be:

Paragraphs 1 and 2 *describe* the *widespread use* of Buzby by the Post Office.

Paragraphs 3 and 4 *explain* the *public's disquiet* with the telephone service. This disquiet, it was felt by the Post Office, made such a campaign necessary.

Paragraph 5 *describes* pilot *research* on the effectiveness of a television advertisement.

Paragraph 6 *compares* the *usefulness in an advertising campaign of the image* of a person and the image of a cartoon character.

Paragraph 7 *continues* the comparison, raising the issue of the appropriateness of *form to content*.

Paragraphs 8, 9 and 10 *describe* in detail the *audience* the Post Office is aiming at and how its public relations people view that audience.

Paragraphs 11 to 15 *describe* the *campaign* in detail.

Paragraph 16 *contemplates* the immediate *future use* that can be made of Buzby through to the following Christmas.

Paragraph 17 *comments* on the *impact* that Buzby has had on Post Office staff and on the public, and includes a value judgement on the success of the campaign.

The first word in italics in each of the above summaries denotes the function of each paragraph, and the second word, or group of words, the content. These different elements of the content combine to form part of the total message of the communication.

This functional approach to the techniques and content of the communication ignores other elements of the message such as style and tone; these also contribute to the final effect upon the reader.

Presenting results

We can isolate function and content from these other elements, and relate them to wider issues in communication, if we analyse the message in the document using the chart in figure 10.

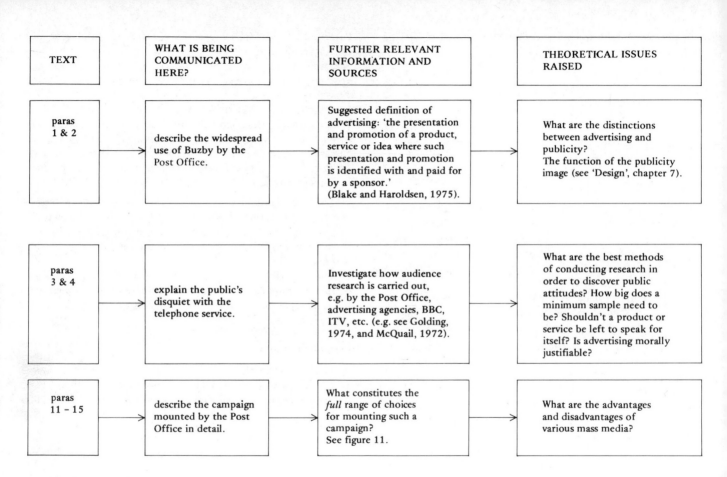

TEXT	WHAT IS BEING COMMUNICATED HERE?	FURTHER RELEVANT INFORMATION AND SOURCES	THEORETICAL ISSUES RAISED
paras 1 & 2	describe the widespread use of Buzby by the Post Office.	Suggested definition of advertising: 'the presentation and promotion of a product, service or idea where such presentation and promotion is identified with and paid for by a sponsor.' (Blake and Haroldsen, 1975).	What are the distinctions between advertising and publicity? The function of the publicity image (see 'Design', chapter 7).
paras 3 & 4	explain the public's disquiet with the telephone service.	Investigate how audience research is carried out, e.g. by the Post Office, advertising agencies, BBC, ITV, etc. (e.g. see Golding, 1974, and McQuail, 1972).	What are the best methods of conducting research in order to discover public attitudes? How big does a minimum sample need to be? Shouldn't a product or service be left to speak for itself? Is advertising morally justifiable?
paras 11 – 15	describe the campaign mounted by the Post Office in detail.	What constitutes the *full* range of choices for mounting such a campaign? See figure 11.	What are the advantages and disadvantages of various mass media?

Figure 10

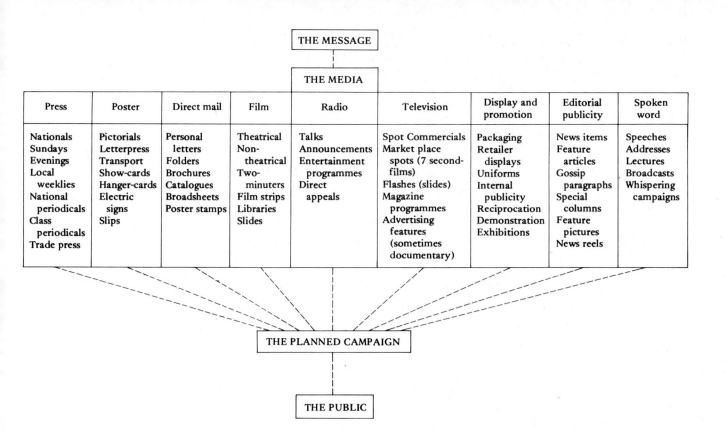

Press	Poster	Direct mail	Film	Radio	Television	Display and promotion	Editorial publicity	Spoken word
Nationals Sundays Evenings Local weeklies National periodicals Class periodicals Trade press	Pictorials Letterpress Transport Show-cards Hanger-cards Electric signs Slips	Personal letters Folders Brochures Catalogues Broadsheets Poster stamps	Theatrical Non- theatrical Two- minuters Film strips Libraries Slides	Talks Announcements Entertainment programmes Direct appeals	Spot Commercials Market place spots (7 second- films) Flashes (slides) Magazine programmes Advertising features (sometimes documentary)	Packaging Retailer displays Uniforms Internal publicity Reciprocation Demonstration Exhibitions	News items Feature articles Gossip paragraphs Special columns Feature pictures News reels	Speeches Addresses Lectures Broadcasts Whispering campaigns

Figure 11

Making connections

An attempt to classify the full range of media available for such publicity campaigns was made by Chandor (1950) and is reproduced here as figure 11. When considering this chart of available media we should note the changes that have occurred since it was published in 1950. Which of the media listed above have become obsolete today because of the availability of other media? If you thus connect and *conceptualize* the case-study material you deal with, you should find yourself beginning to draw up something like a 'theoretical map' of the field of communication studies. In the Buzby example, the route leads from an analysis of a campaign by a large public corporation in the 1970s, through a comparison of advantages and disadvantages of the various mass media, to a consideration of changes in the media. This latter area may well fall into the historical or development section of a communication studies course (as it does in the AEB 'A'-level).

Your ability to make such connections will depend on the width of your own reading, and the guidance you receive from your tutors. We must be careful, however, since communication is such a wide human activity, not to attempt to take in too much country in such maps. If we do we shall defeat the purpose of analysis defined in chapter 1.

You should now tackle the questions that follow (Assignment L) on the Buzby case study, and on completion of your answers reflect on the learning that has taken place by completing the case-study chart (table 1). Note that questions 6, 7 and 8 differ from the others in that they deal with theoretical issues in communication rather than simply with communication skills.

ASSIGNMENT L

(Document 16)

1. You are asked to help arrange a suitable wall display of Buzby material for a school or college or office. What pictures, TV stills or posters would you use? Explain how you would arrange them, provide a key if necessary, and supply suitable captions. State briefly who your presumed audience is and the overall theme of the display.
2. Write a short article of about 300 words about the Buzby campaigns. This can be for a local newspaper or a college magazine, but make it clear which you have chosen to write for.
3. Write the script for an advertising spot for Buzby, to be used on a local radio station. Try to get this recorded afterwards.
4. Using graphic presentation where appropriate, show the use made of television in the Buzby campaigns to date.
5. On behalf of the Post Office Telecommunications consumer relations department, write a letter of reply to Mr S. Brown of 14 The Drive, Rothborough, Northants, who has written to complain that 'the recent Buzby advertising campaigns are yet further examples of the GPO wasting our money'.
6. In note form show what important principles of

communication can be derived from the information in the article and the back-up material.

7. Evaluate the relative importance in the campaign of (a) the Buzby image used; (b) the words chosen for captions; and (c) the design of the advertisements.
8. Suggest outlines for a publicity campaign which intends to make available the facilities of your own school/college outside existing hours for the benefit of members of the public in the county in which your school/college is located.

A framework for studying images

When you have completed the questions on the Buzby case study along with the chart, you should be ready to tackle the wider issues raised by the next piece of material: 'institutional images' (figure 12). This template — developed by John Mundy and Patrick O'Keefe from original work by Richard Dimbleby — can be applied, amongst others, to the following institutions: banks, the armed services, media institutions, schools, colleges, the police and medical services.

The template itemizes, in capital letters, input material, and in lower-case, student assignments and study. The various sources of information on the left of the chart produce an image of an institution (e.g. the police) in the student's view. You should then examine the dominant images that are offered of the institution, and analyse the differences between the input and your own image (i.e. between the image the police intend to present to you of themselves, and the image they actually *do* present to you). This should lead to an investigation of the way that different people's images of the institution vary. (It might be simpler at first to apply the template to your own school or college.) You should also develop here an understanding of *how* an intended image is created by such an institution, and of the *methods* used to convey that image to the public.

We must recognize that as soon as an institution tries to influence or control the image it presents, it indulges in rhetoric, or persuasive communication. Attempting to make people evaluate you in the way you wish them to is precisely the same, in communicative terms, as attempting to make them behave in a particular way — buying your product or using your service. (Dyer (1982) shows how the classical figures of rhetoric, which were originally applied to verbal communication, can be usefully applied to the study of modern visual rhetoric such as advertisements.)

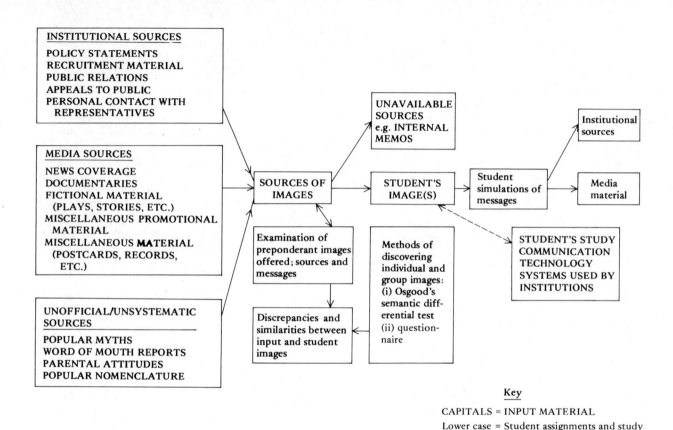

Figure 12 *Institutional images*

Using the framework

Taking the police as an institution and looking, for example, at institutional sources, we could include under 'Appeals to the public' the television programme 'Police Five' and newspaper advertisements placed by the Police Federation in the national press during salary negotiations. A further example would be the police recruiting leaflet dealt with in some detail later in this chapter.

Osgood's semantic differential test (1967), referred to in the template, represents a systematic attempt at measuring the feelings and attitudes that members of an audience have towards certain concepts. His method involves three separate steps:

1. The feelings and attitudes (values) under investigation are expressed in binary form on a 5- or 7-point scale.
2. The selected audience is asked to record its reactions using each scale.
3. The results are averaged.

Baggaley and Duck (1976) used the test to establish semantic differences between a television presenter who addresses the camera directly and one who is caught by the camera in three-quarter profile. The results of their experiment on a small sample audience of twelve are given in table 2:

The results indicate that the three-quarter shot suggests that the presenter has greater expertise, is more reliable, sincere, humane, fair, precise, tolerant, emotional and relaxed.

When evaluating case-study material or presenting project work, the application of this semantic differential test may well aid you in more precise analysis of effective presentation, though you should remain cautious about any results derived from too small a sample.

Table 2

	1	2	3	4	5	6	7	
Ruthless				+----o				Humane
Fair		o----+						Unfair
Imprecise				+----o				Precise
Expert			o-------+					Inexpert
Partial		+o						Impartial
Weak				+o				Forceful
Intolerant				+----o				Tolerant
Cautious					+o			Rash
Unemotional				+----o				Emotional
Intuitive			+o					Rational
Relaxed			o----+					Unrelaxed
Direct		o----+						Evasive
Unreliable				+----o				Reliable
Sincere		o-------+						Insincere

o indicates the presenter caught in three-quarter profile
+ indicates the presenter addressing the camera directly

Barriers to communication

When you investigate the differences between the intended image and the actual image received by you, you should take account of the barriers to communication which might account for the differences between your image and the intended one. Following Parry (1967) we can distinguish these main barriers to communication:

1. *Limitation of the receiver's capacity* For example, X signals are transmitted, X minus Y are received, but receivers may naturally compensate by adding meanings to signs received. One word may compensate for many not understood.

2. *Distraction*
   (a) A competing stimulus (another conversation)
   (b) Objective environmental stress (excess humidity)
   (c) Subjective stress (illness or drugs)
   (d) Ignorance of the medium (inappropriate language chosen)

3. *Unstated assumptions*
   (a) That the receiver already has certain information
   (b) That the receiver is familiar with technical language or terms
   (c) Lack of sensitivity to the listener's level of understanding
   (d) Withholding of certain necessary information

4. *Incompatibility of schemas*
   (a) A mental framework derived from past experience which governs the interpretation of new information
   (b) Incorrect cultural assumptions about the receiver

5. *Intrusion of unconscious or partly unconscious mechanisms*
   (a) Projection
   (b) Identification
   (c) Repression

6. *Confused and ambiguous presentation*
   (a) Typography inappropriate
   (b) Syntax inappropriate
   (c) Medium of communication inappropriate

7. *Absence of communication facilities*
   (a) Rhetorical questions
   (b) Groups too large for effective communication
   (c) Excess of information channels

We should add to the above list:

8. *The stereotyping of the receiver by the sender and viceversa.*

The above itemization of 'barriers to communication' fits in with the view that human communication consists primarily of the transmission of existing messages, where the meaning exists in the sender's purpose, prior to the communication process; rather than in the process of interaction between sender and receiver, or between message and receiver. If the original message is not transmitted effectively, we should look, in this view, for the cause of this failure in a barrier to communication which stands between sender and receiver. Or, as Parry puts it, these 'postulate a situation where a sender is trying to convey a message to a recipient, the failure being traceable to one or the other parties or possibly to both'.

In the light of this classification of possible barriers to communication, we can now consider an example which could form the content for our template 'institutional images'. The following recruiting advertisement, Document 17, was published by the police to encourage people to apply to join the police force.

Boase Massimi Pollitt Univas
COI - Police - COI 5406
Daily Mirror - w/c March 16
7/7 mono - 1 bromide
FINAL PROOF

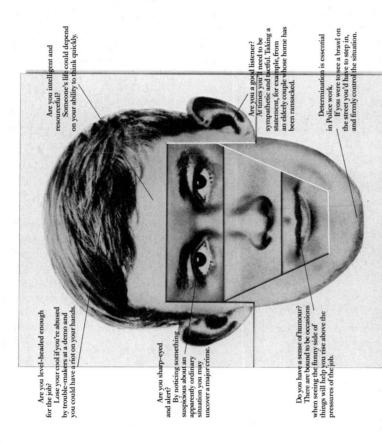

Are you wanted by the Police?

Are you intelligent and resourceful?
Someone's life could depend on your ability to think quickly.

Are you a good listener?
At times you'll need to be sympathetic and tactful. Taking a statement, for example, from an elderly couple whose home has been ransacked.

Determination is essential in Police work.
If you were to see a brawl on the street you'd have to step in, and firmly control the situation.

Are you level-headed enough for the job?
Lose your cool if you're abused by trouble-makers at a demo and you could have a riot on your hands.

Are you sharp-eyed and alert?
By noticing something suspicious about an apparently ordinary situation you may uncover a major crime.

Do you have a sense of humour?
There are bound to be occasions when seeing the funny side of things will help you rise above the pressures of the job.

As you can imagine, not everyone who wants to join the Police is up to the demands of the job.

But for those men and women who do have the personal qualities we look for in every Officer, there are prospects of a challenging and rewarding career.

Starting with ten tough weeks at Police Training School, followed by two years on the beat.

You'd begin on £4,956 if you're under 22, £5,919 if you're older.

In London you'd be on £6,438 under 22, £7,401 over.

It's exactly the same for women as for men, and there are equal opportunities for promotion as well.

Fill in the coupon and we'll send you our brochure.

Then, if you think you're the sort of person we want, send us an application form. The chances are we'll bring you in for questioning.

To: Police Careers (England and Wales).
Dept.DM/00126 Harrow Road, London W2 1XH.
All vacancies are open to men and women.
To join you must be a British subject, fit and at least 18½. Men must be at least 5'8" (172.cms).
Women 5'4" (162.cms).
I am in full time education □   I am a Graduate □
Name (Mr/Mrs/Miss)
Address
Date of Birth

POLICE OFFICER

IF YOU'VE GOT A LOT TO OFFER US, WE'VE GOT A LOT TO OFFER YOU.

79

ASSIGNMENT M

(Document 17)

1. Apply to this advertisement the classification techniques introduced in dealing with the Buzby case-study material in order to identify its elements.
2. What, if any, unstated assumptions are implicit in the advertisement?
3. When reading the advertisement, what (if any) competing stimuli tend to distract you from the task?
4. What (if any) prior assumptions from your own past experience of the police lead you to interpret the advertisement as you do?
5. Which (if any) aspects of the typography, syntax or mode of presentation do you find ambiguous in the leaflet?
6. Which (if any) examples of stereotyping of the receiver are present?
7. Which (if any) examples of confusing rhetoric are present?

This assignment on the police recruiting advertisement constitutes only one aspect of work on institutional images. We have moved from considering, in chapter 2, case-study material which requires a period of approximately three hours to complete, through various shorter assignments that introduce theoretical considerations, to an example of institutional images involving student activity for many hours of work, possibly for a number of weeks.

This assignment also indicates the depth to which it is possible to go using case-study material. Whether you actually work to this depth will depend on whether the emphasis of your work is on the detail of individual images or on the overall concept of the image of the institution.

Thinking about practice: specific

We next want to extend our thinking about the processes of communication in which case-study work involves us. Some case studies require you to assimilate and analyse material and to demonstrate that you possess certain skills by using the material. Other case studies go beyond these necessary basics and require you to develop the original material in some way, to relate it to communication theory and to evaluate the way in which you have used skills and theory.

A short 'creative' case study

Let us take the following case study as an example. It was included in a study conference for 'A'-level students, and the results and comments of one work group are given:

DOCUMENT 18

(You have 1¼ hours for this assignment)

The production of a newsletter publicizing a local carnival

You are a working party assigned to this task by the leisure sub-committee of the local council.

Audience	Local community
Method of distribution	Put through letter boxes
Medium of communication	Sheet A4 paper, one side; duplicated only in black and white; lay-out and graphics to be determined by working party
Content	Again to be determined by working party, but should obviously include specific information regarding venue, date and activities
Method of working	We suggest that you organize your group so that each member of the team is aware of his/her responsibility within it
Resources available	Stencils Typewriters Glue Scissors Magazines Scrap paper A4 paper Member of staff (available for advice)

NEWSFLASH!

You have just received a telephone call. A colleague has discovered that tomorrow's edition of the local newspaper is to carry an editorial expressing concern over the exorbitant cost to the rate-payer involved in the mounting of the local carnival.

Comment

As our later detailed analysis of the work shows, the task here involves more than the demonstration of skills necessary to physically produce the carnival newsletter. You have to demonstrate also your ability to work in a group, to apply your knowledge of one area of the mass media (a local newspaper), to decide upon the most effective response to the local paper's criticism of the work you are doing, and to select the most appropriate medium for that response.

Using your knowledge of the mass media, you have to imagine and develop some of the case-study material yourself. In this respect the case study is creative rather than purely analytical in content.

An analysis of success and failure, and of the learning that took place in attempting the above task, might run like this:

An analysis of one working group's results

Medium: Specified

Content: Not specified

Use of time: In the relatively short amount of time available, we consider that our group spent far too much time (a) discussing content; (b) discovering that all five members of the group were never going to reach unanimous agreement on content; (c) finally organizing a method of determining content. An alternative to our tried system would be for one person alone to produce a draft leaflet in (say) twenty minutes; within this time the group should vote on it and abide by the majority decision. This would allow the group more time for the production and design of the newsletter — after all, this is what will finally be communicated to the audience, not the group's discussions! This should result in a far more professional finish than we achieved.

We wasted time here also because we were all misled by the instructions. Simply because the brief stipulates: 'Content to be determined by working party', this does not necessarily mean that everyone has to be involved from the outset all the time. On reflection, the group agreed that *part* of our problem was caused by the pressure of time, and part because we started *doing* before we had adequately analysed all of the processes involved. We latched on to the idea of dividing the work up among different members of the group — which is obviously essential — but spent an excessive amount of time actually doing this. We discussed this far too fully and democratically given the limited amount of time available. One of the main barriers to effective group communication here was our lack of experience of group work with a relatively large number of people, and having to work under such pressures. We now ask ourselves just how realistic the time limit was. We appreciate the necessity of tutors imposing some time limit to simulate reality, but question whether any working party ever has to work to such a deadline for this sort of event. Another problem arose from the tutor's relative reluctance to help us in the task. This was due to the necessity of our learning from practical experience of the problems involved in the communication. The tutor's ability to offer advice does not arise from her expertise as a media practitioner but from the fact that she is forewarned of the aims and problems involved.

Did our group need someone in charge who would constantly emphasize the pressures of time and assume overall responsibility for delegating different tasks from the outset? Some of us now think so. Two or three of us should have been prepared to adopt this role, even at the risk of appearing temporarily unpopular with the others in the group (see chapter 5). The group could then select who it wanted to do this job. We should each reflect on and write notes on how we would diplomatically but firmly deal with such a problem next time it arises. (It's undoubtedly the sort of communication problem that occurs frequently in industry!)

In spite of the above reflections, we don't feel that the final product (p. 83) was entirely valueless.

The basic idea of using the bus as the design is a good one. It allows us to present a lot of relevant information to our audience, information that it wants. But is the final product more like a poster than a newsletter? (A newsletter should include more information.) Our chosen design reduced the amount of information we could physically include.

The other problem with the bus formula is that it tends to emphasize the venue rather than the content of the carnival. The fact that it is taking place at the bus station is relatively marginal compared with the information about the events taking place at the carnival.

Further, our invention of Kojak to open the carnival was a hasty and inappropriate decision — overkill if ever there was! Our choice of time (in the absence of any specification here) is not particularly realistic either — why did nobody in the group spot this fault? Float processions don't usually start when all the Saturday afternoon shoppers are returning home!

There are other loose ends in our communication too. 'Fancy dress', for example, means very little to a member of the public who doesn't even know how to enter the competition — no follow-up information for the public is provided here. Also we have not included timing for the different events. We should have remembered that our audience can be split into groups with various interests. One last point: we could

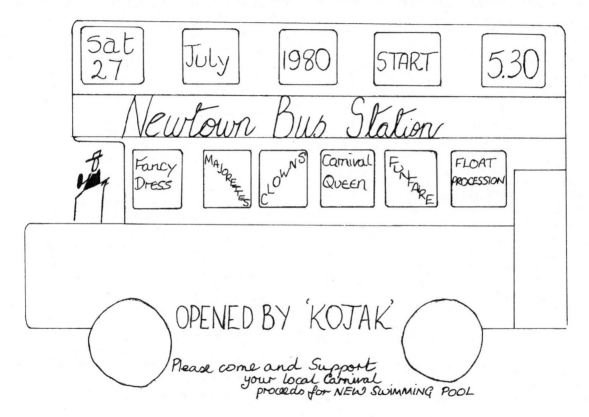

83

have done this job so much better (though not in 1¼ hours!) if we had been allowed to use *both* sides of the paper!

ASSIGNMENT N

1. Allowing your group two hours for completion of the task and using both sides of a sheet of A4 paper, redraft the newsletter.
2. Tape-record as fully as you can the oral communication that takes place within the group while it is completing the task.
3. Analyse the oral communication that takes place, identifying in particular the effectiveness of the structures for completing set tasks, communication between individuals in the group, and barriers to communication.
4. Evaluate the effectiveness of your second draft in comparison with your first.

Thinking about practice: general

Whether you have completed a 'short' or a 'long' task, an 'analytical' or a 'creative' case study, it is essential to ask yourself the following questions about the learning process you have been through. Some of these are the same sort of questions you will later be asking yourself about your project work, the focus being your own diary/report on your project. This is covered in chapter 6.

1. Why did I succeed and fail to the extent that I did in solving the problems of communication that occurred in the case study?
2. Were my problems primarily of my own making or caused by external factors?
3. Was my initial approach to the problem a failure because (a) I failed to clarify the nature of the assignment; (b) I failed to identify relevant methods of collecting information to complete the assignment; (c) I failed to locate sources of relevant information; (d) I failed to collect all relevant information; (e) I failed to organize all the relevant information I had collected for the specified communication purpose?
4. Did I fail to correctly identify the relevant principles on which an appropriate approach to the task was to be based?
5. Did I fail to consider relevant alternatives to my original idea for solving the communication problem?
6. Why did I opt for (say) alternative 3 rather than 1, 2 or 4? On reflection choice 2 would have been better because . . .

7. Did I fail to apply all the basic terms and concepts to the task that I could have done, or did I become too involved with the completion of the practical tasks at hand to the exclusion of learning from the process.

8. Did I identify clearly all the potential barriers to communication involved in the task?

9. Was I sufficiently aware of possible injected values and ideologies involved in the communication?

10. Which models of communication could I have applied to the task to deepen my understanding of the communication process further?

11. What aspects of the work involved in this task amounted only to repetition and involved no new learning?

12. Did such repetition reinforce my understanding of the theoretical issue(s) involved?

13. Did such repetition simply bore me, presenting me with no new angles or understanding of principles?

14. Was I given all the data necessary for successful communication?

15. To what extent was I expected to introduce my own ideas to develop the given data?

16. To what extent were the audience, medium and message predetermined?

Where we are

We have reached the end of part one of this book. In part two we look at project work. But before we do, it will be useful to attempt to summarize and chart the stage we are at. Box A in the following chart (figure 13) represents the particular case-study material we have included so far in this book. Boxes B, C, D and E represent the communication terms, skills, principles and models we have covered up to now. Box K represents the project material included in part two of this book, and boxes F, G, H and I the communication terms, skills, concepts and models that arise. Box J adds some general theoretical consideratons about the usefulness of models of communication.

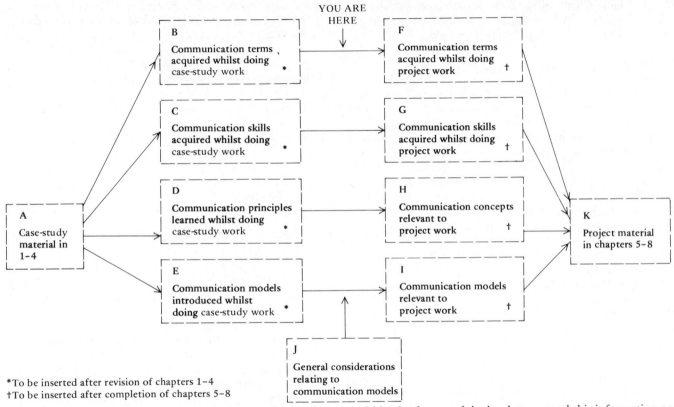

YOU ARE HERE

B Communication terms acquired whilst doing case-study work *	**F** Communication terms acquired whilst doing project work †
C Communication skills acquired whilst doing case-study work *	**G** Communication skills acquired whilst doing project work †
D Communication principles learned whilst doing case-study work *	**H** Communication concepts relevant to project work †
E Communication models introduced whilst doing case-study work *	**I** Communication models relevant to project work †

A Case-study material in 1–4

K Project material in chapters 5–8

J General considerations relating to communication models

*To be inserted after revision of chapters 1–4
†To be inserted after completion of chapters 5–8

Note The above division into boxes represents a division for the purposes of clarification only; in no way should they be taken to represent absolute division in practice between the different areas of work. Since we do not have the space within the format of the book to expand this information on a single page, this first page represents the key to which later pages refer.

Figure 13

Thus at this stage in this book we should be able to identify the understanding we have gained by completing boxes B, C, D and E as follows:

B. Communication terms acquired whilst doing case-study work

Actor	Intrapersonal
Addressee	communication
Addresser	Interpreter
Advocate	Mass communication
Audience	Medio communication
Barrier to	Medium
communication	Message
Broadcast	Method
Channel	Motif
Channel noise	Narrowcast
Code	Non-verbal
Collocation	communication
Communicatee	Perceptual dimension
Communicator	Purpose
Content	Receiver
Context	Referent
Decoder	Register
Destination	Sender
Dialect	Semantics
Encoder	Semantic noise
Feedback	Sign
Form	Source
Gatekeeper	Style
Interpersonal	Symbol
communication	Syntax

C. Communication skills acquired whilst doing case-study work

Skim reading
Noting of key words, main points and phrases
Writing summaries to specified lengths
Production and presentation of rough drafts and final copies
Preparation of scripts for radio interviews
Role play using a radio script
Writing of press releases
Analysis of visual material for the significance of message content
Production of possible examination questions on case-study material
Writing captions to photographs
Writing a magazine article to a specific length
Writing a formal letter as a secretary to an organization/society
Writing a letter to a member of the public as a public relations officer
Preparation of notes for speech
Diagrammatic representation of differing elements within a single audience
Developing material consistent with a given theme/original material
Evaluation of newspaper articles by given criteria
Mounting an exhibition
Arranging a wall display
Script writing for a local radio advertisement
Production of newsletter

D. Communication principles learned whilst doing case-study work

The first principles on the list are essential for setting up the communication; the later principles involve increasing sensitivity to the communication process and imply an understanding of those barriers and cultural differences that affect it.

1. Definition of the primary purpose of the communication. Definition of the secondary purposes of the communication.
2. Definition of the intended effect upon your audience.
3. Definition of the audience; and distinctions within the audience by age, education, attitude, social class and knowledge of subject matter.
4. Definition of the essential content of the message.
5. Selection of the appropriate channel/medium for the transmission of the message.
6. Selection of the relevant and significant from the irrelevant and insignificant elements in the message.
7. Definition of the appropriate length of the communication.
8. Definition of the context/physical constraints in which the communication is to take place.
9. Definition of the role (if any) I am asked to play in the communication.
10. Evaluation of the audience's familiarity with the channel, medium and technology I will be employing.
11. Evaluation of the appropriateness of the message to the audience.
12. Evaluation of the appropriateness of the channel, medium and technology to the audience.
13. Estimation of the amount and nature of feedback likely to occur from the communication.
14. Evaluation of the extent to which meanings in my message are likely to arise (a) from the message itself; (b) from the nature of the audience; and (c) from the nature of the context in which the audience receives the communication.
15. Evaluation of the extent to which I am likely to be able to use feedback in order to improve the formulation of my message.
16. Definition of the symbols, signs and codes I am using; for example, does my message carry explicit meanings or are my meanings implicit, requiring audience activity to render them explicit?
17. Definition of the relation between primary and secondary meanings in the communication. Are the latter aiding or adversely affecting the former or vice versa? To what extent can secondary meanings that interfere with primary ones be jettisoned?

18. To what extent has the relationship with my intended audience been thoroughly and sensitively developed during the communication?
19. Definition of the extent to which the symbols, signs and codes I am using are culturally specific (thus leading to possible failures in communication).
20. Evaluation of the applicability of my case-study practice to the particular theories and models of communication.

E. Communication models introduced whilst doing case-study work

Lasswell: mass communication
Shannon and Weaver: transmission of messages
Schramm: encoding and decoding
Gerbner: perception
Westley and MacLean: gatekeeping
Osgood: semantic differential test

J. General considerations relating to communication models

Models of this kind generally do little more than stress some very simplified and general notions, often in such a boldly graphic manner as to impair the student's consideration of complexity, context and change. (Corner and Hawthorn, 1980, p. 7).

And:

Like any other approach to theory, building models demands a degree of sophistication in students which many will not possess in the early stages of a new course. There's a danger that the apparent clarity provided by a model may mislead students into over-simplifying what, in reality, are complex acts of communication. Nevertheless, students can take some of the first steps up the ladder of abstraction by applying simple models to their own activities. If those can be planned in careful sequences, they may well illustrate stages in the building of a model, or changes that a dynamic model would allow for. We've already seen how concepts of audience, for example, can arise from a survey of the press, from preparing materials for named audiences, from interviews, from devising questionnaires, and so on. In addition, as one of the teachers suggested, simple check lists, or grids, devised by the students and teachers, can provide systems for more thorough analysis of activities. The extraction of models, and their development, can hopefully be consolidated by regular reviews (say, once a month) of all activities and productions (written, oral or audio-visual), so that students get in the habit of standing back from their work and seeing if the building of models has thrown any light on their own problems and difficulties. Perhaps, in this way, students can begin to draw their own theory maps, as they gain clarification from the analysis of practical work. (*Communication Studies: B — The First Term*, The Schools Council, 1978)

Communication models

Advantages

Give us an idea of complicated objects and events in a general way.

Enable us to see how the particular communication event fits into the general pattern.

Provide a classification for an order and nature of events.

Suggest new ways of looking at old problems and familiar events.

Provide a structure of reference for purposes of study.

May take a variety of forms, diagrammatic, verbal, statistical and mathematical.

Are useful if we are clear as to the reasons why we are applying a particular model to the material studied.

Are useful if we are clear about what we hope to derive from the application of the model to the material.

Can highlight particular features of the material and show how these features relate to each other.

Disadvantages

Can misleadingly over-simplify complex events.

Lack precision, preventing precise understanding.

Confuse the reality of communication with the models themselves.

If applied to an inappropriate situation, tell us more about the model than about the situation.

Can tend to close down the investigation of complex material.

May claim a comprehensiveness that can never in reality be achieved.

Can misleadingly make simple events seem complex!

Looking back

When you have completed each Assignment you should ask yourself the following questions:

1. What tasks was I actually involved in during my work on the assignments?
2. To what extent did I arrive at a solution to the problems?
3. How were the solutions (to the extent that I found them) arrived at?
4. Why did I reject the solutions I did reject?
5. Were my reasons for rejecting these solutions valid in the light of subsequent work?
6. Where did I fail to apply principles of communication which were in fact relevant?
7. Which theories and models should have been applied to further help me analyse and explain the data presented in the assignments?

PART TWO PROJECTS

AN INTRODUCTION
TO PROJECT WORK

5

Directions in project work

If the classroom is the focus for communication theory, all that happens outside in the 'real world' provides possible raw material for project work in communication.

Somebody who once 'taught' me English literature wrote as the first sentences of his book on Shakespeare: 'We go to the great writers for the truth. Or for whatever reason we go to them in the first place it is for the truth we return to them, again and again' (Danby, 1961).

In communication studies you return to the classroom so that you can discuss and reflect upon the communication processes that you have experienced while doing your project work. Of course, you live in that world all the time, but the beauty of project work is that it admits that the 'real' world outside is just as important as the academic world (which some teachers still believe is the only place where true learning takes place).

Project work allows you much more freedom than you normally have in the real world, or on traditional academic courses. You can work on your own, or choose to work with student colleagues who share your interests. On many courses you can choose your own subject area, and often break new ground by doing original research. You have the chance to make regular connections between college/school, and the outside world.

On many courses — and certainly on the type this book focuses upon — project work lays as much emphasis upon *how* you communicate and *how* you become aware of communication as upon the production of the final product (the artefact).

Project work is going to involve your development as a 'social being' more than most traditional types of classroom learning. The extent to which you so develop will depend on how conscientiously you try to carry through the aims of your project as specified in your original terms of reference. How much you learn of the principles and processes of communication is in turn going to depend on how conscientiously you reflect on the acts of communication in which you are involved during your project work. The focus for such reflection is the diary/report on the project, covered later in this book.

You and your tutor

A preliminary to effective project work must remain, however, a sound, equal and productive relationship with your tutor. You, as the student, are the one who is going to make the fundamental decisions on your project. Your tutor is there to advise you *if* necessary. In the course of your project work you have the chance of getting to know your tutor much better than in an orthodox teaching situation where the tutor's role is primarily to provide information. In project work the relationship is one of greater equality. The tutor is there to help you overcome or avoid technical problems that may unnecessarily obscure the learning process or affect the completion of the project.

In nearly every case you, the student, are going to end up as a greater expert than your tutor in the project field that you have chosen. Your tutor will be able to offer advice, nevertheless, because s/he will remain more distanced than you from the project material that you will become involved in. There will be occasions when it will be useful to use your tutor as a sounding board for aspects of your project work; you can try out some of your ideas for the effective communication of aspects of your project on him or her. But remember that the tutor in no way replaces the actual audience at whom your project is finally aimed, as specified in your terms of reference.

While you will find it useful to use your tutor in this way, never allow his or her possible enthusiasm for your project to take out of your hands decisions which are rightfully yours, as maker of the project, and which you are quite capable of taking independently.

You should also expect, and be prepared to act upon, criticism from your tutor if it appears that you are way behind an appropriate schedule for the completion of the project — and if you cannot prove that things are in fact otherwise.

You and your colleagues

You will learn even more from project work if you consistently discuss your problems and successes, not only with your tutor but also with other students in your group. There is, unfortunately, a competitive drive in our education system which means that only a certain number of students can pass a particular examination each year. Standards therefore fluctuate from year to year rather than being consistent. This reflects the competitive nature of our generally individualist society which, in schools and colleges, can reduce the cooperation that could help many students to learn more rapidly.

Some students, for example, brought up with this competitive attitude towards learning, won't let others see their notes or marked essays because they feel this reduces their own advantage. But students who for such reasons refuse to discuss their problems and successes with other students stand to lose far more than they gain — since communication is public not secret, and since students are working in different subject areas anyway, merely learning to apply in common the same principles of communication, the compulsion to keep work hidden should be consequently reduced. Everyone has the opportunity to become expert in his/her chosen field.

A project which sees the light of day only at the last minute before the deadline for completion, is far more likely to wilt under the eventual scrutiny of its real specified audience than one which has grown organically in the light of criticism and comment from the tutor and other members of the group.

Project work can avoid many of the disadvantages inherent in those courses where student performance is measured solely by a final examination. Assessment in the project is on-going in many cases — the tutor evaluates student performance from the earliest days of the project. Examinations in themselves can be fallible devices, as Hills (1979) points out:

> The possession of a recognized qualification in a subject at school level is no guarantee that sufficient background to a subject is possessed. This is not intended to be a criticism of work in schools, it is more a basic criticism of the examination system which inevitably must select certain areas of a syllabus to test, but equally must exclude others. (p. 18)

Project work avoids some of these pitfalls, not least because it allows 'feedback' to develop between teacher and student.

> Instead of the process consisting simply of the teacher passing messages to the student, the communication process should be a dynamic interchange with the student feeding back information on how the teacher's messages have been received; as a result he can amplify or extend the communication as necessary. The message channel and feedback channel, therefore, should form a continuous feedback loop between teacher and student so that the student keeps the teacher aware of his difficulties and the teacher keeps the student aware of his progress and attempts to solve any difficulties he may have. (ibid.)

Hills is speaking here mainly of the classroom lecture type of teaching, but this is the relationship that project work should naturally allow to develop.

Thinking about content

When you come to think about the subject matter for your project you should be as *specific* as possible. Students often find themselves in difficulties of their own making in project work because they choose topics — and project titles — that are far too wide given the resources available.

What for example, would be the nature of the real, live audience interested in a project entitled 'Housing'? Who is there who knows nothing at all about housing, but wants to know about it in the general sense that the title implies?

The project that is referred to later in this section, from which the extracts about interviewing are taken, deals specifically with the subject of housing *in Leeds*. Better still, a title such as 'A factual report on the proposals for the redevelopment of Shilhay, Exeter' implies both a specified audience *and* a purpose. The audience, at least, is those people who previously have no such information, and the purpose goes beyond the project itself since it involves a specific issue of importance in the real local world. The title 'Housing' on the other hand, seems merely to imply *a* project. In reality, only a government department, with all its resources, could really do justice to a general title such as this, and such a title would imply the length and substance of a government White Paper on the subject. A student presenting a report with such a title is suggesting that s/he is presenting something wide and authoritative on the subject when in fact s/he is not. (The real audience for government White Papers, it is worth noting, is in fact extremely narrow: Members of Parliament, Housing Officers, media personnel with a special responsibility for reporting on housing, etc. One of the jobs of the latter would be to condense (and therefore 'gatekeep') such government reports to make them accessible to the television viewer, the radio listener and the newspaper reader.)

Some project titles

The 'Shilhay, Exeter', title above is taken from a list of projects submitted by students in 1978 for the AEB's 'A'-level in communication studies. Extracts from the rest of the list (Document 19) will give an idea of the range and type of project work being done for this course.

DOCUMENT 19

Typical project topics

Speech acquisition in children

Symbolism and perception with relation to Fine Art

Ideological hegemony and the media — newspapers and trade-union activity: a report

The presentation of women in the mass media (with an evaluation of public attitudes to this): a report

Non-verbal communication in everyday experience

An information leaflet on 'The single homeless' ('down and outs')

An introduction to hi-fi systems

A young look at an old town — a programme on Bath and its activities

The play's the thing — a guide to encourage theatre among young people

A study of the problems associated with the development
  and operation of Concorde
A guide to the workings of the Stock Exchange
'Korak of the Apes—the attack of the Yor-o-dors': a cartoon
  film for TV
A tape 'walkabout' for the City of Exeter, and supporting
  brochure
A tape/slide presentation, with teacher's notes, to be used in
  a lesson about Oxfam
The weekly newspaper and the community
A guide to switchboard procedure
A guide to the British education system for prospective
  Nigerian students
A report on production techniques employed by an amateur
  and a professional drama group
A booklet on Punks and their place in society
Devising an advertising campaign — promoting a product
West-Indian immigrants and their culture
The selling of George Eliot
Advertising and the corner shop
Working men's clubs
Coventry City football club
Writing as an expression of personality
Communicating with the blind
Development of communication through music therapy
Anarchism — a viable proposition?
An examination of the Beaverbrook empire from its beginnings
  to its present situation
The Greek-Cypriot community in Britain and the problems
  their children face in British schools

DOCUMENT 20

Categories of project

In the AEB's 'A'-level the student has to prepare a project
registration form, in consultation with the tutor, outlining
the scope, aims, objectives and intended readership/audience.

The subject, form or structure of the project are not pre-
scribed. Possible formats are: a leaflet; a booklet; a magazine;
a tape-slide sequence; a short radio programme; a television
programme (or part); a flim (or part); a report (of not less
than 4000 words); a manual; a guide. For audio-visual
formats, length should be not less than ten minutes, and a
script should also be produced. For film and video projects,
a short sample of the completed artefact should be produced,
as well as a storyboard and documentation.

Criteria for assessment

The assessment of the project will take account of:
  the effectiveness of research and classification:
  awareness of audience;
  consistency with and awareness of aims and objectives;
  care with arrangement and presentation;
  sense of structure and lay-out;
  adequacy of audience testing before and after project
  work;
  use of scheduling and planning;
  adequacy of the assessment of the work and of the

student's own performance;

consultation with a person or organization likely to commission the project.

The completed project file will consist of: the work itself; a diary/log of the project activity (including commentary and self analysis as well as a factual record); a written assessment by the student of the work and of the experience, referring to audience testing, criticism of the work, and evaluation of learning about the communication process.

(Group projects are acceptable, provided that each student, when registering the project identifies the contribution s/he intends to make.)

An oral also takes place, consisting of a ten-minute presentation by the student to a group of about five of the student's peers. This includes a description of the project, a summary of aims and objectives, and an assessment of its value and success, followed by questions and answers on the project. Aids may be used in the presentation, which is examined by tutors and moderator.

ASSIGNMENT O

(Documents 19 and 20)

1. Select six titles, about which you know most at present, from the list quoted in Document 19.
2. In the light of the project requirements laid down by the AEB ask yourself how effectively you would be able to produce an artefact under each of these six titles.
3. Ask yourself what would be an appropriate audience for each project title.
4. Ask yourself what resources would be available to you when working on each title.
5. Summarize the process by rating your selected six titles in order of suitability to you.

When you have completed Assignment O you should have a clearer idea of the criteria for choosing a particular project area and of some of the pitfalls to be avoided. If you could answer positively all of the above questions on one selected title then it is possible that you have already discovered an area of work that you could profitably become involved in.

But why, once a student has determined the content, medium, purpose and audience for a project, might s/he still have problems in defining the terms of reference? In your terms of reference you should try to give the examiner marking your project as precise an idea as possible of what your project is, its intention, audience, the resources that will be available, your scheme of work and how you will test the effectiveness of the communication. Throughout you should err on the side of over-precision, rather than leaving areas undefined, while remembering that any later necessary modifications can be made and noted in your diary/report. Substantial modifications should be referred to your tutor and to the moderator appointed by the examining body for the project.

Do not attempt to satisfy the examiners by stating at the outset that you will produce a quantity of material which either (a) you simply do not possess the resources to produce; or (b) is inappropriate because it is superfluous — beware of the danger of overkill! It is possible to fail to communicate through producing too much information as well as too little.

Consider carefully issues of controversy. If your terms of reference commit you to producing a guide, make sure that it merely outlines issues of controversy without the imposition of your own judgements. If you do wish to enter into the controversy in your project, then you should change your terms of reference.

Registering your project

Included next, in Document 21, are some examples of students' completed project registration forms.

DOCUMENT 21

1. *Project title* The past and future of the Grand Union canal
Readership or audience A society concerned with the use of the canal.
Aims of finished project To give the local canal users an insight into the uses and importance of canals in the past and for the future, and into improvements which could be made in the canal system in order to satisfy modern-day needs.
Resources available The canals, literature from libraries, clubs and societies relating to canals in general; museums; the mass media.
Plan of action To photograph and research canals; to produce drawings of the canals showing the improvements which could be made to the Grand Union canal; to contact users of the canal and the local water authority.
Provisional plans for testing the effectiveness of the communication Preparation of a questionnaire for the audience to answer after they have read the project to (a) find out if the information contained in my project has been conveyed; and (b) to make remarks upon my recommendations.

2. *Project title*   Spotlight on the Seventh Day Adventist Church
Readership or Audience   The project is to be aimed at people aged between 16 and 22 who may be students but do not necessarily have a religious background.
Aims of finished product   Many people have never heard of or know little about the Seventh Day Adventist Church and therefore the aim of this project is to introduce and possibly stimulate an interest in the beliefs and objectives of the Seventh Day Adventist Church.
Resources available   The Seventh Day Adventist Church itself, using the help of members of the Church and literature published by the Church. Other resources to be used: recording equipment in the making of the programme.
Plan of action
(a) Collection of information using books, magazines and the help of Church members
(b) Using the information and facts obtained to produce a programme script
(c) Production of a tape/programme using the script
(d) Reproduction of the tape/programme to a target audience and use of questionnaire
Provisional plans for testing the effectiveness of the communication   To allow members of the target audience to listen to the programme and, by using a questionnaire, to test the effectiveness of, and to obtain feedback from, the project.

When completing your project registration form you must take care to be specific. The person reading it must be able to get a definite idea from it of the type and nature of the project you will produce. On the other hand, you should ensure that you don't include an excessive amount of detail. Since no provision is made for you to supply additional information with the registration form, you should aim to provide sufficient information to approximately fill the available spaces on the form in average-sized handwriting.

The next Assignment (P) is designed to give you practice in clarifying your intentions in your own project work.

ASSIGNMENT P

(Documents 20 and 21)

1. Consider the above specifications for project work.
2. Evaluate in class how self-explanatory the two students' project registration forms are. What further information might you require about the students' intentions if you were the examiner/moderator?
3. Write a memorandum to the students asking for any necessary clarification of unclear or ambiguous elements in the specifications.
4. Put yourself in the position of the students submitting the forms and submit to the examiner/moderator redrafts of the registration forms dealing with the points raised in the memorandum.

Varieties of project work

It will be useful now to look at some examples of different types of project work actually undertaken in colleges.

The three Documents which follow (22, 23 and 24), along with Assignment Q, are intended to get you thinking about the nature and purposes of different types of project work. They should help you increase your awareness of the particular type of project work in which you are involved and to relate it to some of the theoretical issues in communication introduced in part one of this book.

These three specifications — taken from an extremely wide field — were drawn up by teachers for students doing project work in general studies and communication on part-time courses in colleges of further and tertiary education. They therefore differ slightly in emphasis from the AEB's 'A'-level specification for project work.

DOCUMENT 22

The stages involved in project work

Undertaking a research exercise and preparing a report

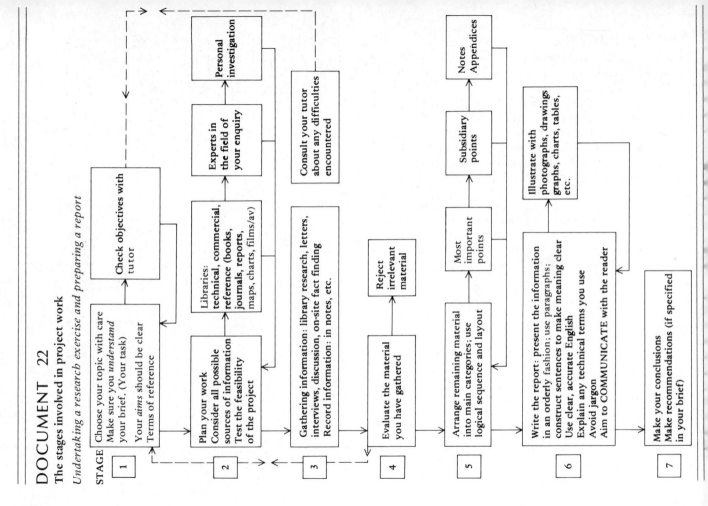

STAGE

1 Choose your topic with care
Make sure you *understand* your brief. (Your *task*)
Your *aims* should be clear
Terms of reference

Check objectives with tutor

2 Plan your work
Consider all possible sources of information
Test the feasibility of the project

Libraries: technical, commercial, reference (books, journals, reports, maps, charts, films/av)

Experts in the field of your enquiry

Personal investigation

Consult your tutor about any difficulties encountered

3 Gathering information: library research, letters, interviews, discussion, on-site fact finding
Record information: in notes, etc.

4 Evaluate the material you have gathered

Reject irrelevant material

5 Arrange remaining material into main categories; use logical sequence and layout

Most important points

Subsidiary points

Notes
Appendices

6 Write the report: present the information in an orderly fashion; use paragraphs; construct sentences to make meaning clear
Use clear, accurate English
Explain any technical terms you use
Avoid jargon
Aim to COMMUNICATE with the reader

Illustrate with photographs, drawings graphs, charts, tables, etc.

7 Make your conclusions
Make recommendations (if specified in your brief)

PROBLEM TACKLING

Given: (A) problem area

Identify problems within area (B)

Select one problem (C)

Does your solution generate sub-problems? (N)

Who is it a problem for? (A)

What would constitute a solution or part-solution of the problem? (E)

What theories can you construct (a) to solve the problem; (b) to assist in working towards its solution? (F)

To test your theories, what information do you have already? (G)

What further information do you need? (H)

How reliable are your sources? (I)

Where can you get this information? (I)

What methods are you going to use to get it? (J)

look at · visit · plans · Vox Pop · write · tape · newspapers · phone · survey · library · film/VTR · local authority · MP · Ask

Combine a theory with information—is it good enough to reinforce it? Reject it? (K)

Formulate a proposition or propositions for the solution or part-solution. (L)

What do you do with your proposition? (M)

Nothing · Convey it to relevant authorities? · What is the best way of doing this? · Do something about it yourself?

103

DOCUMENT 24

Project work

1. *Why do project work?*
   The aim of project work is to give you the opportunity to study in depth a particular topic that interests you or annoys you, and to reach a point of view about it which you can justify in detail. Project work enables you to work on your own initiative and to use a range of methods.

2. *Topics*
   The topic you choose to work on must be:
   (a) something on which you have a *point of view* to present, or something on which, after further work, you will have a point of view to present;
   (b) *social* (i.e. something affecting more people than just yourself);
   (c) *controversial* (i.e. something not purely technical and/or descriptive).

3. *Groups*
   You can work either in groups or individually, but the topics will choose the groups rather than the groups the topics.

4. *Targets*
   The target is to produce your point of view on the topic chosen, taking into account to the maximum extent possible other points of view.

5. *Materials*
   There are two main sources for other people's points of view on a particular topic:
   (a) primary, i.e. people's experiences and views that have *not* yet been turned into books, films, tapes, television programmes, songs, etc.
   (b) secondary, i.e. people's experiences and views that *have* been turned into the above.
   Your work will need to take account of both sources, but (a) will often be far more interesting and exciting than (b).

6. *Form*
   (a) Written and illustrated, including use of surveys, etc.;
   (b) tape-recorded (for example, a twenty- to thirty-minute programme);
   (c) any combination of (a) and (b);
   (d) any other possible form you suggest by agreement.
   Whatever form you choose you should acknowledge fully the use you make of secondary material.

7. *Presentation*
   Although you will be specializing in a particular area, please aim to make your work as intelligible as possible to those without specialized knowledge.

8. *Assessment*
   Assessment will take into account the following factors: content, originality, critical element, organization and presentation, acknowledgement and use of sources, language.

9. *Suggested workplan*
   (a) Choose topic;
   (b) choose groups;

(c) choose form(s);

(d) break down project into parts, considering available materials;

(e) hand in outline of work for approval, letting me know, in advance if possible, what materials and facilities you may need.

My job is to give you any help possible in your work, so don't wait until the project is due to be handed in before raising problems. Consult me, by arrangement, at any time during class and at any reasonable time outside of class.

ASSIGNMENT Q

(Documents 22, 23 and 24)

1. Discuss the above project specifications in class.
2. Consider in each case whether the emphasis appears to be on the production of the final artefact from the project work, or on the learning from the process of communication. Bring forward reasons for your conclusions. With which groups of students might each type of project be used?
3. Suggest how the layout of each project specification might be improved to increase the clarity of the communication.

Approaching your project

When you start project work you should choose first the content/message you wish to convey and pinpoint the audience at whom you wish to aim that content. Only when these are decided upon should you select the medium most appropriate for conveying your content/message to that particular audience.

You should consider seriously as many alternative media as possible and leave your choices open for as long as is practical. It is useful to try out sections of the work in practice before you complete any registration form for the project, since this will commit you to certain specific decisions.

When working on your project you will inevitably discover that its form affects the content. Its basic form must be kept to, but if you come to the conclusion that you have made the wrong choice, you should work out, and note in your diary/report, the reasons why you think this. (You should be prepared to answer questions about any such changes in the oral examination if there is to be one.) If you find that you have to make changes in the style of your project, or in the number or type of illustrations you will be using, note and evaluate the possible effectiveness of all such changes in your diary/report.

Organizing the project message

The message you want to convey in your project is more likely to have maximum impact if it arouses a *strong*, favourable or hostile, emotional response from your audience. The search for such a strong response should not, however, be followed so diligently that the *content* of your message and your purpose in the communication is obscured. You should also remember that elements that provoke such a response will only have such an effect if they are used sparingly; if such devices are used too frequently their impact is severely reduced.

You should take account of the fact that the order of presentation of material in your project will affect the response of your audience. Audiences tend to remember those elements delivered at the beginning and end of the message more clearly than those in the middle. This might, in certain projects, constitute an argument for including in the middle section those elements which are likely to develop a strong response, since this may compensate for the tendency of your audience to be less receptive here. The assumption that your audience is more receptive at the end than in the middle depends upon their knowing the approximate length of the presentation, or upon your clearly signalling that the end is approaching. In an oral presentation this may be done by your saying such things as 'before I conclude I would like to say . . .', or by your inclusion of recapitulation. Recapitulation of earlier elements is valuable in addition since it complies with the advice often given to speakers for effective oral communication: *say what you are going to say, say it, and then say what you have said*. This precept should not be ignored in written communication.

Any elements of your message that *can* be actually presented, should be, rather than merely being referred to. In the case of a written project, for example, it is better to include an extract from the article referred to (possibly a photocopy of the original), rather than simply to summarize it. This assumes that the space is available for you to do this, and that you possess the copyright holder's permission to do so. An additional advantage for many projects is that the inclusion of such material makes it possible for you to break up a page of text which might otherwise, in appearance if not in fact, be boring. On the other hand you must come to a decision about the value of uniformity of appearance in your project, since for some, such uniformity is an essential element. The virtues of variety in presentation must be balanced against uniformity by reference to overall purpose.

In projects where inevitably you will be identified as a person with a message (in the presentation of a tape-slide sequence, for example, as opposed to a written project), you must consider yourself as an element in the message. You should evaluate the extent to which your own personal appearance when presenting the slides, voice characteristics on tape, etc., will aid or hinder effective presentation of the message in your project material.

Repetition of material in your project should encourage retention of the message, if retention is your aim. Remember, however, to balance such repetition against the possibility of boring your audience with over-familiarity with your material.

If one of your aims is that the audience should actually learn from your project, you should consider the inclusion of elements which will enable them to be active and participate, since this is more likely to be effective than leaving your audience purely passive.

Audience attitudes

Take account of the attitudes of your audience. If you intend to reinforce and develop its existing attitudes you are invariably going to have a much simpler task in communication than if you are attempting to change an existing attitude. Remember that your project will be assessed on the *process* of communication that you develop and not simply on the rapidity with which the audience receives the communication. A project that attempts little will achieve little, whereas a project that attempts systematically to analyse and change audience attitudes may achieve little but may receive much credit for developing an appropriate approach.

Your audience will be inclined to expose itself to those aspects of your message with which it is in sympathy and resist the impact of the elements to which it is hostile. It will carry a certain number of expectations, associating certain elements of a message instinctively with others, and expecting, therefore, to make a certain response.

Your individual audience member will be most receptive to those messages which tend to reinforce his/her own image of his/her self and least receptive to those which tend to disrupt that image.

Different elements in your audience will exhibit differing receptive capacities. Broadly speaking, the younger the audience the more open its response and the quicker the reaction to your message will be. This factor is basic, however, and is relevant only in the case of an audience which is comprised of a cross-section of the public. If you are aiming your project at a specialist audience, the specialist nature of its knowledge will tend to obliterate the distinction between younger and older sections, since the more open response of the former may be neutralized by the greater degree of information on the subject possessed by the latter.

You should take into account the following factors when considering the nature of your audience: its average age; whether it is mixed by sex or not; the occupation or type of occupation of the majority; its income level; its level of education; its special leisure interests. You should also consider what your audience is likely to know already about the content of your project and whether it is likely to be sympathetic or hostile to that content. You should attempt to discover what (if any) has been the reaction of previous similar audiences to similar project content. You should also consider whether, for your specified audience, controversy or argument is likely to enhance or hinder your communication of the content. It is also worth considering here what economic, social and political factors have given your audience the characteristics it has, and the personal reasons that have led you to select such an audience.

A checklist of questions about your project

Before you start, during, and at the end of your project work, you should pause, distance yourself from your project, and ask yourself the following questions:

Before you start — practical issues

Is the subject likely to remain sufficiently interesting to sustain my interest throughout the whole of the period that I shall be working on the project?

Is the subject of sufficient importance to the intended readership or audience for my project to justify the amount of time I will be investing in the project?

Am I well enough equipped to tackle the project? (Or can I at least see myself in the short term developing the necessary ability to complete the project work?)

Do I have access to the research material necessary for the completion of this work? Do I live sufficiently near to the research facilities that are available?

Am I sufficiently free from other commitments (academic, personal, etc.) to make effective use of the research facilities that are available?

Within my college or school course, does my timetable make it possible for me to fulfil the project tasks I shall want to do?

Is my project likely to illuminate interesting work in other directions which could lead me to neglect my main objectives?

Are any parts of my project likely to involve expenses I am unlikely to be able to afford?

Are any of the locations I would need to use impractical?

Is my project likely to extend my abilities but not become impossibly difficult?

Is it going to be possible for me to test parts of my project for effectiveness on samples of my intended audience? (The great advantage of testing parts of your project is that you can incorporate any necessary changes into later parts of your project work.)

Am I likely to be able to stick closely to my terms of reference? i.e. is my audience likely to be able to get from my project what I stipulated it should get?

While you are working

Is my technique of accumulating information from my identified sources imperfect? Am I, for example, reading whole chapters of books of dubious relevance to my subject when I should be using alternative reading techniques? (Consult Buzan, 1981)

Am I arranging the information I am acquiring in the most suitable way for the average audience member who will eventually see my project? Am I retaining in my mind's eye a clear image throughout of the nature of my audience?

Is there sufficient variety in my presentation of material (for example, in a written project, between text and illustrations)?

Is the juxtaposition of different types of material or presentation going to aid or interfere with the audience's understanding? Or is my presentation likely to appear monotonous and boring to the audience?

Are the different elements of the project contributing naturally to the achievement of a unified final effect?

Does my introduction lead naturally into the body of the project? Can I see how the work will develop towards the conclusion I intend? Am I guilty of repetition of material? If so, what is the cause of this?

Am I guilty of unjustifiably expanding my material in order to meet (say) a minimum word limit for the project? Alternatively, am I being insufficiently selective in pruning material which is not strictly relevant to my theme? Am I likely to go way over any maximum word limit?

Am I distinguishing sufficiently between problems of content and problems of expression?

Am I noting, and accounting for (in my diary), any discrepancies between the project I specified in my terms of reference and the project I am actually producing?

Wider questions

What general points about my subject do I intend to communicate in my project?

What are the major and minor concepts I wish to get across?

In what context will my audience actually receive the communication?

Will I control to any extent the physical situation in which they will receive it?

Am I expecting my audience to be active or passive when receiving the communication?

What is my audience's present level of knowledge about the subject matter?

What medium or combination of media is most suitable for my subject matter and audience?

How has my project subject matter been handled already by the medium or media I intend to use? How has it been handled by other media? Is the subject matter already so well covered that there cannot possibly be any real originality in my project? What can I learn from viewing previous attempts at handling similar subject matter in the medium or media I have chosen?

How does the audience I have chosen respond to similar communications?

Will the major concept that my project carries be standard or new to my audience? Is this concept too demanding, or insufficiently demanding, of my audience's level of understanding?

How important is my project likely to be to my chosen audience? Will it relate strongly or weakly to the audience's social, aesthetic, psychological or intellectual needs?

To what extent is the major concept in my project likely to be culturally disturbing or neutral to my audience? How will I be able to reconcile the requirements that my project should be entertaining, educational and informative? How will I avoid any entertaining element degenerating into trivialization of my subject matter? How will I avoid the educational element becoming propaganda, and any technical element becoming esoteric?

To what extent are the project's concepts likely to be distorted by the process of communication itself?

ASSIGNMENT R

1. Change the written checklists above into a different form using words *and* diagrams or charts.
2. Compare the effectiveness of your product with the original checklists.
   (*Note* For further information about the methods our minds use in retaining various presentations of information, consult Buzan, 1981.)

PROJECT DIARIES/REPORTS

6

Requirements and aims

In project work the process of doing the work is of equal value to the artefact which is finally produced. It is during the process that your understanding of principles, theories and practical skills in communication must take place. The writing of a diary/report (referred to as a diary from here on) on your project provides the focus for such understanding. The AEB's 'A'-level in communication studies, for example, stipulates that: 'At the end of each course each candidate must present a personal project file. . . . Each project must be accompanied by a short assessment written by the student of the objectives achieved and the problems encountered.' But even if your course makes no such stipulations, it will benefit your understanding of the process of communication in which you are involved if you do keep a diary as you work.

You should start to keep a diary as soon as you begin to think about your project, and as you write it up keep the following questions constantly in mind:

Are you carrying out enough research into the nature of your audience?

Will the final product you are working towards really suit the audience's needs and capabilities and raise its level of understanding?

Are the audience's emotional or cultural needs producing problems of communication; and how are you dealing with these problems?

Are you really making use of all available relevant sources of information — verbal, visual, graphic, auditory?

Are you choosing the most appropriate length, tone, style, symbols for your particular audience?

Are you organizing and arranging the material in the most appropriate manner?

Are you developing a clear idea of the sort of feedback you will attempt to obtain from your audience? What possible problems are likely to occur?

What possible alternatives are there to the decisions you have actually taken in developing your project?

Some diaries on projects fail in their main aim of developing the student's awareness of his/her own practice of communication. Consider the following extract from a diary that was a relative failure compared with the standard achieved by the project itself. The chief cause of failure here was simply the *brevity* of the diary. Length appears to exert the same influence on project diaries as it does on personal diaries. If you decide to keep a personal diary in order to find out more about yourself, you are more likely to achieve this objective if you commit yourself to writing a certain amount each day (and probably at a regular time, too). You will feel some compulsion to record and analyse feelings, thoughts, etc. because you have to fill (say) a page a day. The same seems to apply with project diaries. You will find out more about the process of communication your project involves you in if you commit yourself to writing a certain total amount by, approximately, the end of each week, more frequently if possible. You should, however, write only as events of communicative significance occur in your work. Size, not only medium, can affect the message.

Diary extract I

> This project diary is a summary report rather than a full diary. I found it very difficult to make full reports on the problems I had encountered, difficulties of research and limitations and abilities as a communicator. After solving the problems I did not feel like writing them down again.

This last sentence implies that all the problems in the project work were faced up to and solved and that keeping a diary consists solely of writing these problems down.

It is quite possible that this student was simply faced with a lack of time in which to complete his diary. But the writing of it should on no account be left until near the end of the total time allowed for completion of the project. You should aim to include entries in your project diary every week *at the very least*. This will help you to mull over your successes and highlight your failures — the latter is more important, since this can enable you to change and improve the later parts of your project work. Your diary should never consist of your simply writing down problems, though this is an essential. At its best it should include (a) an attempt to describe the problem; (b) an attempt at explaining why it occurred; (c) an evaluation of how successfully you as a communicator faced up to it; and (d) an indication of how you would go about solving a similar communication problem should it arise again in the future.

Let us now consider an extract from the student's final project work: 'a series of leaflets, each with a common introduction' aiming 'to explain supplementary benefit in a simple and satisfactory form' for 'current, new and prospective claimants'. This should give us a measure of the relevance of his comments in his diary to the project work he eventually produced. Document 25 is one leaflet he produced to be printed as an A5-size folded 4-page leaflet.

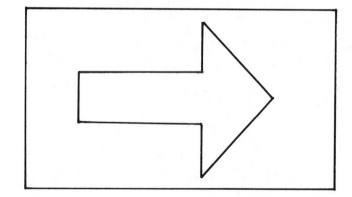

DOCUMENT 25

WHAT IS SUPPLEMENTARY BENEFIT?

IT IS AN AMOUNT OF MONEY THE GOVERNMENT HAS DECIDED YOU NEED TO LIVE ON EACH WEEK.

IT INCLUDES:
1) AN AMOUNT TO COVER YOU AND YOUR FAMILY'S ORDINARY NEEDS, SUCH AS FOOD AND CLOTHES.
2) HOUSING COSTS, SUCH AS RENT AND RATES.
3) ANY EXTRA EXPENSES WE CAN ALLOW.

BENEFIT CAN BE PAID IF FOR ANY REASON YOU ARE NOT ENTITLED TO UNEMPLOYMENT BENEFIT, OR IF YOUR UNEMPLOYMENT BENEFIT IS LESS THAN THE AMOUNT OF MONEY THE GOVERNMENT HAS DECIDED YOU NEED TO LIVE ON EACH WEEK.

YOU SHOULD MAKE A CLAIM FOR SUPPLEMENTARY BENEFIT IMMEDIATELY, BY OBTAINING FORM B.1 FROM YOUR UNEMPLOYMENT BENEFIT OFFICE, WHO WILL THEN SEND IT TO YOUR LOCAL SOCIAL SECURITY OFFICE. WE WILL THEN WRITE TO YOU ASKING YOU TO COME INTO THE OFFICE FOR AN INTERVIEW.

ON THE NEXT TWO PAGES A ROUGH GUIDE TO THE AMOUNT OF SUPPLEMENTARY BENEFIT YOU MIGHT RECEIVE IS GIVEN.

YOU MAY HAVE EXTRA NEEDS, SUCH AS HEATING FOR DAMP ROOMS, OR WE MAY HAVE TO MAKE SOME MORE DEDUCTIONS, FOR EXAMPLE: A WORKING SON OR DAUGHTER LIVING AT HOME, WOULD BE EXPECTED TO GIVE YOU SOME MONEY TOWARDS RENT COSTS.

YOUR NEEDS:

MARRIED COUPLE	£29.70
SINGLE PERSON-	
PAYING RENT/OWNER-OCCUPIER	£18.30
OTHER PERSON AGED 18 OR OVER	£14.65
OTHER PERSON AGED 16-17	£11.25

INSERT THE AMOUNT WHICH APPLIES TO YOU IN BOX 1.

IF YOU HAVE CHILDREN, FOR EACH ONE ADD ON:

AGED 13-15	£9.35
AGED 11-15	£7.70
AGED 5-10	£6.25
AGED UNDER 5	£5.20

INSERT THE TOTAL IN BOX 2.

IF YOU PAY RENT AND RATES, INSERT THE AMOUNT YOU PAY EACH WEEK IN BOX 3.

IF YOU ARE AN OWNER-OCCUPIER, DIVIDE YOUR YEARLY RATES AND MORTGAGE INTEREST (NOT CAPITAL REPAYMENTS, AS THIS IS A FORM OF INVESTMENT), BY 52 TO GIVE A WEEKLY FIGURE. TO THIS ADD ON £1.00 FOR REPAIRS AND INSURANCE. INSERT THIS AMOUNT IN BOX 3.

IF YOU ARE LIVING IN SOMEONE ELSE'S HOUSEHOLD, ADD ON £1.70. INSERT THIS FIGURE IN BOX 3.

BOX 1
BOX 2
BOX 3
TOTAL   THIS IS ROUGHLY THE AMOUNT OF MONEY THE GOVERNMENT HAS DECIDED YOU NEED TO LIVE ON EACH WEEK.

DEDUCTIONS.

ALL OTHER SOCIAL SECURITY BENEFITS, SUCH AS CHILD
BENEFIT AND UNEMPLOYMENT BENEFIT.

INSERT THIS TOTAL IN BOX 1.

ALL PART-TIME EARNINGS OVER £2.00, (£6.00 IF YOU
ARE A SINGLE-PARENT FAMILY).

ALL OF YOUR WIFE'S WEEKLY EARNINGS OVER £4.00.

ALL OF A WORKS PENSION OVER £1.00.

ALL OF ANY OTHER MONEY YOU MAY RECEIVE EACH WEEK
OVER £4.00.

INSERT THIS TOTAL IN BOX 2.

SAVINGS

NO DEDUCTION IF YOUR SAVINGS ARE LESS THAN £1250.

IF YOUR SAVINGS ARE MORE THAN £1250, YOU CAN
STILL CLAIM BENEFIT. TELL YOUR SOCIAL SECURITY
OFFICE HOW MUCH YOUR SAVINGS ARE, WE CAN THEN
TELL YOU HOW MUCH MONEY WILL BE DEDUCTED FROM
YOUR BENEFIT EACH WEEK.

BOX 1
BOX 2
      TOTAL   IF THIS AMOUNT IS MORE THAN
THE TOTAL ON THE PAGE OVERLEAF, YOU MIGHT NOT
BE ENTITLED TO BENEFIT - YOU SHOULD STILL CLAIM.

IF THIS AMOUNT IS LESS THAN THE TOTAL OVERLEAF,
THE DIFFERENCE IS PROBABLY THE AMOUNT OF BENEFIT
YOU WOULD BE ENTITLED TO - MAKE A CLAIM NOW.

Comments on diary extract I

A fuller diary on this project might have made comments such as the following:

> Practical considerations affected the amount of information that can be included in the leaflets. It is perfectly reasonable, in terms of the overall effectiveness of the communication, to concentrate attention upon the average audience member. But this tends to discriminate against those members of the audience who *would* be able to handle more information, against those who would want to claim allowances for mortgage interest and capital and heating, and against those who would be able to readily understand relatively brief information.
>
> Satisfying the needs of the majority of the audience and saving public money naturally appears the most reasonable approach to take, rather than going out of the way to satisfy the needs of the minority who might be justified in claiming the benefits but will consequently receive them later than they should. The practice of aiming at the majority of the public and possibly neglecting minorities tends to be followed in communications from large firms, government departments and the mass media itself.

The diary reveals that a government desire to save 'public' money — even at the expense of a minority of claimants — is the motive force in determining what bits of information should be excluded from such leaflets. Practical considerations of space affect what to include; and we have from the student a clear statement, based on the experience of working in a government department, of the thinking behind such decisions (a clearer statement than we are likely to get from an interview in the mass media with some professional gatekeeper who may be concerned to conceal the political and moral thinking behind such decisions).

It would have been far better here if the student had himself teased out in his diary the implications of withholding certain information from claimants and related this to the effectiveness of the communication overall.

In this diary there were insufficient insights into the *process* of communication that took place, since the student's premise regarding the amount of work he would put into the diary effectively prevented him from including more than a few brief comments on the *process* which produced this otherwise useful and impressive project.

Full expression in your diary is the condition for the deepest possible appreciation of the theoretical issues raised by your own project work. Your concern must be to explain and evaluate the process in which you are involved in the communication as fully as possible and in an organized manner.

Diary extract II

This next extract from a student's diary *does* get to grips, through its analysis of the process of communication, with some of the principles and issues involved.

'Countesthorpe College: an introduction and a defence' was a written project aimed at 'parents of prospective pupils' of this state secondary school, and the diary extracts cover the period 15 February to 1 March 1980 inclusive (the project was due for submission by the beginning of April).

The college was opened in the early 1970s and in its early years attracted controversy. The local press, led by the *Leicester Mercury*, focused attention on some of the edu-cational initiatives taken by the college's first principal and supported some of the criticisms made of the college by parents of students and by local councillors. An enquiry into the running of the school was called for and held. The student who produced this project attended Countesthorpe during the late 1970s and felt then that it was still suffering unfairly from the image it had acquired earlier.

15 February Whilst rooting through the school library I discovered a selection of Open University case studies on Countesthorpe College. These made interesting reading since they offered an outside opinion of the college's controversial history. I was in need of this kind of 'distanced' material, because most people I have spoken to so far have been directly involved with Countesthorpe in one way or another; they are therefore biased and defensive. I realized that it would be difficult to write in a fair way about the college since I too feel strongly defensive about the college. So far I have tried to gain knowledge of different opinions about the college so that I am aware of all the arguments when writing a defence of the college.

25 February Meeting with parents (assessment of readership) I have today met parents for and against the college. Arranging the meeting was more difficult than expected, nevertheless it has all worked out. From this meeting several points have been made. I have realized exactly how strongly people feel about Countesthorpe and how their attitudes would not be changed by discussion. They seemed to have a barrier to the sort of communication I was putting forward, probably through previous experience governing the interpretation of the message; therefore there would seem to be an incompatibility of schemas preventing acceptance of my ideas.

26 February Whilst standing at the bus stop I overheard a conversation between two middle-aged mothers. They discussed the education that their children would obtain from Countesthorpe College and expressed concern for their children's educational and emotional (psychological) development. At the expense of appearing rude I ventured to join their conversation by commenting on my own experience of the college. They were interested in my account of the college's educational facilities and surprisingly asked me questions about the controversial issues, i.e. violence, vandalism, smoking and teaching methods. These are the kind of things I was thinking of dealing with in my introduction and it made me feel more certain of the need for such material.

For the first time I really understood how strange the college must appear to people who have been educated in grammar schools, etc. and to people who have had little contact with the school for many years. Although these mothers cannot be taken as representative of the whole community, it does give me some idea of what the audience is like, and what they want to know. It is quite difficult to write something for a wide diverse readership, but it is very important to assess their needs and relate to these in the most appropriate way. Further meetings with parents of prospective children, on an arranged basis, would be beneficial in determining the audience type, and a questionnaire would be useful to determine their needs. From studying other leaflets I have an idea of the type of language to use. Plain straightforward words and short sentences would be best, so as to put forward the message (communication) clearly and unambiguously, but not over simply.

The interest many people have shown in my own experience of the college has made me decide to write about the college's principles as I have found them. This personal angle, rather than textbook reflection, would perhaps hold and sustain interest in the material.

28 February Meeting with prospective parents and students For the first time I met the parents of new students all together. I have previously met many through my research into audience demands and I have got to know some of them well — they then felt more at ease to tell me their fears, if any, of the college's principles. Most parents were willing to listen to the discussion about the college, but some were quite rude and desperately tried to find loopholes in the college's system. Some parents even criticized the college strongly, without having much knowledge of the college at all. The meeting was useful to determine the readership I must cater for.

Another consideration which came out of this meeting is that many people could not remember in detail what the *Leicester Mercury* had said; they in fact had a general impression built up over continuous reading of articles with adverse, bad publicity to the college, therefore detailed analysis of individual articles would be less important than an overall discussion and consideration of the *Mercury*'s treatment of the whole Countesthorpe situation: an analysis and comparison with the national newspapers' treatment would be valid to expose the sensationalism in the treatment by the *Leicester Mercury*.

1 March Throughout the project I have tried to be as fair as possible and to consider all attitudes and opinions in order to give an informed and balanced argument. For this reason I found it difficult to know what to write about in this connection. I knew that people would question my claims about education and I tried to be as explicit as possible. I have come to the conclusion that not everyone is going to agree with me, or what my introduction says. Opinion cannot be changed easily, and I do not feel I have the expertise to persuade people at this stage. Writing persuasively is an art which not everyone has, and I acknowledge this limitation as a communicator.

Not only is the subject of education bound up with opinions and past experience but with politics too. In Countesthorpe's case, some say it was used as a political football to draw attention to a particular party.

Comments on diary extract II

This extensive extract from a student's diary highlights the following general points:

(a) The necessity to be constantly alert to all new possible sources of material, whether books, people or newspaper libraries.

(b) The value of quoting, given appropriate permission and acknowledgements, relevant material originated by others; this can lend an air of authority to your work.

(c) The necessity of paying detailed attention to the organization and layout of your material once you have gathered it.

(d) The necessity of aiming at conciseness in your use of language and illustration.

(e) The possibility of building up your project, adding, deleting and amending material in drafts as appropriate, rather than attempting to produce the entire artefact in one sequence from beginning to end.

(f) The necessity of relating the practice of the communication you are involved in to your theoretical understanding of communication principles and models.

(g) The importance of constantly referring to your aims in your project and evaluating your own practice in the light of these aims.

(h) The need to measure constantly the process of your project against the nature and needs of your audience.

(i) The need to confront the problems of bias, fact and opinion in your material, particularly in those projects which deal with controversial subjects (see chapter 7).

The comment made by the student on 15 February indicates what a diary involves in developing the student's consciousness of communication: 'I was in need of this kind of 'distanced material'. This redresses the drift towards that close identification with project material that occurs for most students (and indeed most authors!).

The extract from 26 February, describing the encounter at the bus stop, indicates the active and social nature of project work in communication and some of its distinctions from traditional academic work. The student might well have reflected further here that by this stage her researches were making use of both formal and informal methods and channels of communication. Her formal methods involved library research and visits to the local newspaper; an example of informal methods is the spontaneous incident described above, where the good journalist with an 'ear to the ground' unexpectedly came across some relevant and eventually publishable material. It is a mistake to assume that learning will only take place when you want, expect, or set up a situation in which you intend it to take place.

The differences between formal and informal channels of communcation have been described in the following way: formal channels of communication are based upon inter-personal interaction between people with common interests or purposes. As they are regularly used, such channels tend to become reliable and stable. Within informal channels we can distinguish between spontaneously formed and auxiliary channels. In the first case, messages are transmitted between participants who for the most part are not aware of the social status and identity of the other participants. These sorts of channels develop, for example, during a period of intense public interest — normally reticent individuals are stimulated by the circumstances to exchange messages with others previously relatively unknown. In the second case, the participants establish networks built around personal friend-ships or purposes. 'The roles enacted in auxiliary channels are not fixed in custom nor defined in law. These sources are evaluated largely in terms of personal reputation of the participants for honesty, knowledge, sound judgement and "connections"' (Shibutani, 1966). Most interpersonal com-munication takes place in these auxiliary channels.

Information and news that is transmitted via informal channels is referred to as informal or unverified news. The interpersonal network of any person will naturally vary from situation to situation and from person to person. If all of the networks linking *all* people are considered, the picture becomes too complex to be comprehended. However, it is possible to view the network from the viewpoint of *one* topic and *one* participant.

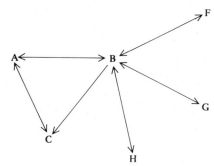

Figure 14

In figure 14, the student, B, meets at the bus stop, by chance, the parents, A and C. There is no prior communicative purpose to the three of them being there, but this spontaneously formed channel conveys the message to A and C that B is a relative expert on the local college. This is because she is both a student at the college and is involved in producing a project on it. B then takes on the role of a central communi-cator, with a higher than average rate of message interchange.

Her contact with the parents leads her later to organize a meeting with parents to discuss her project — a formal communication channel. B may have had contact with other parents, F, G, H, etc. who, before they go to the meeting arranged by B, are unknown to A and C and to each other. As a result of B establishing this formal channel, auxiliary channels of friendship, based on their common interests in the college, may develop between A, C, F, G and H, etc.

The higher contact of the central communicator may be due to the social position held or to psychological factors. Berlo (1960) points out that some occupations and positions in society are more communication prone than others: 'These include receptionists, salemen, barbers, elected politicians, waitresses — people whose role behaviour increases their contact with others'. (However, some people adopt these central roles because they have certain *psychological* wants, such as the desire to be needed, or for attention.)

As you work on your project you are establishing for yourself, within that particular field, the role of central communicator.

In this particular diary we note that the entry on 26 February reveals a close appreciation of the needs of the student's audience: 'This personal angle rather than textbook reflection would perhaps hold and sustain interest in the material'. She is choosing between a variety of approaches, and in doing so, using information about her audience — obtained almost accidentally — to help her in selecting the most suitable approach for her audience.

Her entry for 28 February indicates the extent to which she has already begun to work out ideas for testing the effectiveness of her project. And at this stage, as the parents disagree, she reflects fruitfully on the differences between fact and opinion and on the existence of those political assumptions which may act as a barrier to communication.

(During your project work, it is necessary to reflect regularly on how the concepts listed elsewhere in this book relate to the experience of communication with which you have been involved.)

She then comments on the different ways that people acquire information, putting forward the view that if they acquire general impressions about an issue only over a long period of time, then there is little point in trying to change these general impressions by presenting detailed articles; an 'overall-discussion' treatment might be more effective.

As a theory of communication this does not necessarily hold, but the student's approach of trying to draw conclusions from particular experience with the aid of communication theory indicates a productive approach.

(The thinking behind this book is that if you appreciate the particular examples included here, you will be able to recall and apply the theoretical points they illustrate to the other situations you will meet in your own project work. Thus the student's diary report on Countesthorpe College should trigger off recall of the points you should take account of when writing your own.)

Most important, this student makes a thorough attempt to evaluate her own strengths and weaknesses as a communicator, reflecting, for example, on 1 March, that her problem is to write of a controversial and complex subject in 'a concise and relatively simple form . . . . Writing persuasively is an art which not everyone has, and I acknowledge this limitation as a communicator'. Perhaps she is being a little modest here;

one cannot logically assign all failures of communication to deficiencies on the part of the communicator. There is a range of other factors to be considered too: unavailability of suitable media, channel noise, the nature of the subject matter, etc. It is possible, indeed, that even the most experienced professional communicators — and in most cases they acquire, rather than are born with, such skills — would find it extremely difficult to persuade large numbers of this audience to change their views, whatever the techniques employed. Some of the views held by parents would be based upon deeply held ideological and political conviction and might never be modified. The parents of some of the children due to go to Countesthorpe may believe, for example, that a stratified educational system which favours the middle class is the only viable education system. The above project, even if it displayed perfect understanding of its audience and exemplary techniques of persuasion, would have little effect on such parents.

The view that all problems and conflicts in society are caused by inadequate communication finds expression in the belief that all you have to do to eliminate all disputes in industry is to improve communications. This view is based partly on the indisputable fact that communication in industry certainly can be improved; and partly on the state's and the employers' vested interest in pretending that there is no real economic or class basis for the disputes that do occur. Improved communications cannot, in themselves, eliminate *all* conflicts, though it serves one side's interests to pretend that this is all the problem consists of.

Pitfalls to be avoided in project work

The following reflections (Document 26) were contributed by the student who wrote the diary extracts on Countesthorpe College. They were written about a year after she had completed her project and shortly after she had taken up a post on a newspaper as a trainee journalist. It is useful to compare the analysis she made of her shortcomings during the project with her later reflections, written when she had become more distanced from her project work. Her diary already shows that she was aware of this problem of distance, but it fails to emphasize sufficiently the problem of distinguishing between matters of fact and history on the one hand, and of opinion and judgement on the other. Her choice of project topic should have enabled her to reflect more deeply on this problem. Inevitably, she failed to cope with all the problems that arose when tackling this difficult topic. However, her own, somewhat modest, diary comments prove that her determination at least led her to encounter such problems productively.

DOCUMENT 26

Some of the problems I faced when working on my project are the same problems I now face every day of my life as a newspaper journalist — the collection and analysis of information and the communication of it in a suitable form.

In project work you are given a very wide range of subjects and media to choose from and at first it is easy to get carried away with ideas for ambitious projects which attempt to say something very profound.

Only as time passes — and quickly (!) — does it become all too apparent that as 18-year-olds we often lack the expertise or technical ability to carry out our first intentions.

Such, I am afraid, was my experience. In choosing a subject I opted for an introduction to, and a defence of, Countesthorpe College, a radical comprehensive school, much criticized by the press.

Being a student at the college, I thought I knew everything about its workings and I felt fiercely loyal to its aims and principles. However, as I collected more information from the 'other side', i.e. the press and disapproving parents, I realized that they had a case, and my opinions of the college changed. This is where I ran into dire problems, for how could I possibly defend a system which I began to feel was not quite as perfect as I had earlier believed?

Things became very complicated as I dug out the history of the college and discovered that the criticisms of the college were quite justified at that time. I therefore set out to defend the college for the changes that had been made and the improvements now apparent. Here again I was not entirely successful because I could not entirely defend the college's achievements.

In short, I had been too ambitious in my aims, and chose a subject which required some degree of knowledge of the history of education and psychology; alternatively I could have written a simple report on the workings of the college.

The moral behind my experience is that when choosing a project topic you should try to keep it simple and within your capabilities. Choose a subject which you already know quite well, or which you are very keen to know about, and research it thoroughly.

Another tip is to be selective about the information you collect; you can 'cheat' a little if necessary by including only what you want to include, so making the case lean your way.

Similarly, in the choice of a suitable medium for your project, don't be too ambitious. Don't select radio or film if you seriously lack the technical ability to produce these media.

Bear in mind, too, the relatively small amount of time you have for research and for the assessment of the effectiveness of the project. I can assure you that the time really flies by with often very little really achieved until the last few weeks, when bad planning might leave you working under very heavy pressure.

Finally, I must emphasize that the project can be a lot of fun if you tackle it in the right way. Never lose sight of your original aims and audience and remember that information and the ability to communicate are powerful things.

Ambition is admirable, but a realistic approach spells success — and fewer headaches!

ASSIGNMENT S

(Document 26)

1. Represent diagrammatically the above advice on 'pitfalls to avoid' when doing project work.
2. Identify and discuss any distinguishing features in the account that indicate that the writer is a journalist rather than a current student.

Organizing a schedule for project work

In the process of keeping your diary you will have to select what is relevant from the vast amount of information to which your project has exposed you. Essentially your diary represents your attempt to relate your practice of communication in your project to your understanding of communication principles and theory. Just as the traditional personal diary is used for the planning of future events, so should you use part of your project diary to organize future project activities. And just as the personal diary provides a record of the past, so a summary of your previous week's work provides the basis for the planning of future project work. Certain pages of the diary can be reserved for the writing of such 'minutes' and the planning of future activities (see figure 15).

Figure 15 represents a development of Richard Hare's scheme for planning project work. His book *Know-How: A Student's Guide to Project Work* provides a wealth of information and advice on the practical and technical aspects of project work. Although published in 1970 and now somewhat dated, it should be extensively consulted on the practical/skills aspect of project work.

The sub-headings within Hare's book are as follows: 'Doing a project'; 'Getting yourself organized'; 'Getting your subject organized'; 'Writing letters and taking notes'; 'Using libraries'; 'Interviewing people and making surveys'; 'Using tape-recorders'; 'Using cameras'; 'Presenting your results orally'; 'Presenting your results visually'. There is little emphasis throughout the book, however, on the concept of audience, that key concept which focuses attention on the *process* of communication. Emphasis upon audience leads

A *Work done on project last week (date):* . . . .

. . . .

B *Evaluation of work done last week:*

  (i) Skills learned/developed last week: . . . .

. . . .

  (ii) Principles of communication to which last week's work relates:

. . . .

  (iii) Models of communication to which last week's work relates:

. . . .

C *Work planned for (date) next week:* . . . .

D *Work planned for (?) weeks ahead (date):* . . . .

E *Detail of work:* . . . .

. . . .

. . . .

F *Aspects of project that need revision:* . . . .

. . . .

G *Technical equipment needed for above work and when required:*

. . . .

Figure 15

to a constant consideration of the appropriateness of the communication, rather than solely of the final product of the project work.

One of the virtues of Hare's book is its coverage of a wide range of practical considerations and techniques relevant to areas other than written projects. The book provides information about the use of photography, film, tape-recording, etc., but of course it cannot demonstrate techniques. It should be *consulted*, rather, as this equipment is being used—although technical developments in certain fields mean that it is now necessary to consult more recently published material, such as manufacturers' handbooks or specialist magazines.

The book you are now using concentrates upon *written* projects because it *is* a book. Principles and models of communication can be related here to printed material since we can include such material much more easily than material of other media, which we simply cannot represent. When in the foreseeable future the student may receive audio-cassette recordings or film as case-study material rather than printed matter, then the best way of relating principles and models of communication to that material will be to use material other than print. The limitations on the more rapid introduction of other material are economic. In this respect money directly affects the availability of media.

The next chapter of this book covers in detail some central skills and concepts in project work. But before moving on, you should tackle the next Assignment (T) which focuses attention on the differences between standard projects and projects in communication, and upon the diary's role in emphasizing that difference.

ASSIGNMENT T

In chapter 1 of his book Hare writes:

Project work is a highly responsible form of study. Firstly you have to organize yourself to conduct extensive and penetrating investigations into various subjects — working either on your own or as a member of a team. Then you need to build up your information — gleaning facts and opinions from as many relevant sources as possible. And finally you should aim to produce your own judgements — informative, balanced and interesting reports for presentation orally or in written form.

Thus, 'Doing a project' means that *you* have to decide that information you need; *you* have to work out how best to obtain your material; *you* have to assess what to keep and what to discard; *you* have to plan the best ways of compiling and presenting your eventual report.

This paragraph suggests that there are three functions of project work:
 (i) organizing research;
 (ii) building up information;
(iii) producing judgements.

1. Similarly, identify three functions of project work suggested in this present book.
2. Discuss to what extent the functions identified in 1 coincide with, or differ from, Hare's functions for project work. Suggest reasons why this should be so.
3. Discuss how far (a) the principles, and (b) the models of communication introduced in this book could be introduced through another medium (e.g. tape-recordings, film, tape/slide sequence).

CONCEPTS AND SKILLS IN PROJECT WORK

7

Introduction

This section introduces some central concepts and skills which arise in projects, by taking particular examples from actual project work. The examples relate to those concepts and skills that most commonly occur; you should attempt in turn to relate the general points which are developed from these examples to the project work with which you are actually involved. You should compare these examples with the communication concepts and skills you face in your own project work and reflect on the problems that you need to tackle. It is impossible, given the width of the field, to cover more than some of the main concepts and skills here; these are included to stimulate your own general understanding and practices as a communicator.

This chapter covers first the concepts of selection, bias, ideology and language code; and second the skills of designing, interviewing, obtaining feedback during project work and of working in groups.

Ideology

Issues surrounding the question of selection arise as soon as research for project work is begun. You will find it useful here to try to learn by example and consider the approaches that others have taken to the issues, and to attempt to discern from their work the methods they employed and the problems they were aware of.

We will first take an example of extended written project work: *Magazines Teenagers Read* (Alderson, 1968). Although much more extensive than the work you are likely to undertake, in final form and in approach it is probably far closer to your own level of work than many of the academic textbooks you are likely to use as secondary sources. Such academic textbooks can rarely serve as useful models for your work since audiences and purposes are often ill-defined. Alderson's book, however, is specific in these matters and I shall include examples of its approach in order to introduce the related issue of ideology. Intimately tied to the issue of selection is that of point of view and ideology: what is the point of view, the outlook, the 'system of ideas' held by the researcher and author that leads her to use certain material and reject others?

Alderson's book concentrates on an analysis of *Trend, Jackie* and *Valentine*, magazines aimed at teenage girls. To quote Bernstein's preface to the book, it

> is the result of twelve years teaching of so-called non-academic pupils in secondary-modern schools and day-release classes in colleges of further education. Her book is an angry book, with few holds barred, written by an extremely able and sensitive teacher. It does not claim to be sociological, neither does it meet the demands of the

social survey. Yet I suggest that it will spark off more systematic study by those who have public funds and two or three years to think and do. Mrs Alderson's book was written under quite other circumstances.

Magazines Teenagers Read started life as a 'special study' (rather like a project) on an in-service course at a teacher-training college. It is the approach of this type of book, rather than that of the alternatives to which Bernstein refers, that will be most useful to you when doing project work.

Document 27 is an extract from Alderson's book. In arguing her point of view here, she first extracts and condenses the views of her opponents in order to criticize them, a method you should always follow when dealing with controversial subject matter in project work. Alderson is here criticizing the entrenched interests of many powerful people who work as professionals in the mass media. She maintains that such people often take a patronizing view of the general public and tend to lower educational standards.

DOCUMENT 27

There is a tremendous idealistic potential amongst young people but this is not fostered by the cheap superficiality of the comics and magazines which are produced for one reason alone, and that is to make money for the publishers. Norman Collins of ITA has a very poor conception of public demand. He says:

If one gave the public exactly what it wanted it would be a perfectly appalling service. . . . The overwhelming mass of the letters we get are illiterate, they are ungrammatical, they are deplorably written, and what is more distressing, they evince an attitude of mind that I do not think can be regarded as very admirable. All they write for are pictures of film stars, television stars, or asking why there are not more jazz programmes, why there cannot be more programmes of a music-hall type. I hold the teachers very largely responsible if that is the attitude of people in their teens and early twenties. If we provided simply that it would be deplorable.*

To hold the teacher responsible is scarcely fair while television continues to give the viewers 80 per cent hotch potch of trash. Mr Cecil King of the *Daily Mirror* is quite honest about this opinion of the reading habits of the British public:

The trouble is the critics imagine the great British Public is as educated as themselves and their friends, and that we ought to start where they are and raise the standard from there up. In point of fact, it is only the people who conduct newspapers and similar organizations who have any idea quite how indifferent, quite how stupid, quite how uninterested in education of any kind the great bulk of the British Public are.

It is pointless to refute these statements even though one is loath to believe in it, but the sales of the *Daily Mirror* and the ratings for the lowest common denominator type of programme show that there is truth in them. The question for every teacher is how long are we prepared to accept the two nations; how long are we prepared to accept so called 'high' and 'low' culture. (pp. 111–12)

*Although this remark was made only a few years ago it is interesting to note how out of date it appears — no mention of pop; and jazz, which has earned its place as a serious art form, is lumped together with music hall.

Alderson goes on to argue that the fundamental reason for the existence of these two nations is an education system which was segregating children into different schools at eleven years of age and sending the majority out to become workers on leaving school at fifteen. She argues that if 'taste' for what is 'good' has begun to develop by the age of sixteen it can be reinforced; but if it has not then the child becomes vulnerable to all that is bad in the mass media.

Alderson states that 'comics and magazines are produced for one reason alone, and that is to make money for the publishers'. Now while it is true that this economic motive underlies all such private publishing in our society, it does not follow that this is the *sole* motive behind publication. In addition to the particular desire to make money is the general desire that these readers should be entertained. In that sense the publishers can argue that they are making their money only because they are responding to an effective demand from the public. Collins believes that teachers are responsible for the decline in literacy standards. He apparently ignores the influence that the mass media might itself have on such standards (see Leach, Document 5), assuming that what happens to a pupil during his conscious hours at school constitutes the only influence on such standards. He puts forward the view that there are certain attitudes of mind which are admirable, and that there are others which are distressing.

Alderson agrees with Collins that there are such standards, but argues that the responsibility for their lowering must largely be borne by, for example, television, which 'continues to give the viewers 80 per cent hotch potch of trash'. Collins believes that only formal educational influence is an influence while Alderson argues that television tends to create its own demand which it then supplies. King maintains that this standard cannot be raised because the great bulk of the British public are 'quite uninterested in education'.

Alderson's footnote accepts Collins's notion of status in culture, but maintains that he is wrong to place jazz, 'a serious art form', alongside music-hall. Her belief is that powerful as the mass media are, education, provided there is no segregation at the age of eleven, is sufficiently powerful to overcome these forces. She accepts that culture may be 'high' or 'low' but wants the 'high' to be made accessible to all through a reform in the education system.

We have, in fact, had such reforms since Alderson's book was written, but since we have simultaneously witnessed radical increases in the availability of the mass media, we have not yet seen the improvements in literacy standards which all the participants in the above debate desire.

Common sense

All accept as a matter of ideology that certain activities are more 'worthy' than others; that the values produced by education are more valuable in general than those produced by the mass media. The disagreement between Alderson and King and Collins, for example, does not result from their having different ideologies (i.e. different systems of ideas, 'common-sense notions'). Theirs is in the nature of a tactical disagreement over how to achieve the same objective. Since it is only a tactical disagreement it is possible for them to argue the point—they can communicate. The disagreement between them is over the influence of television on prevailing standards of literacy. Both accept that literacy is to be aimed for since they believe it to be 'organically necessary to our given social structure', to borrow Gramsci's (1971) phrase.

Gramsci made a distinction between those ideologies that are 'organically necessary' and those that are 'arbitrary, rationalistic or "willed"'. 'To the extent', he argued, 'that ideologies are organically necessary they have a validity which is "psychological"; they "organize" human masses, and create the terrain on which men move, acquire consciousness of their position, struggle, etc. To the extent that they are arbitrary they only create individual "movements", polemics and so on . . .'

The view that education and literacy are valuable has a long pedigree in our society; it has taken on the character, in Gramsci's sense, of an 'organically necessary ideology'. There has been an organized struggle over a long period to promote and acquire education and literacy; the fact that the vast majority of people now subscribe to these values does not prevent them remaining as ideologies. Since they are not questioned by most people in our society, they take on the appearance of 'common sense'.

But 'common sense', as Nowell Smith (Hoare and Nowell Smith, 1971) has pointed out, is the 'way a subordinate class in society lives its subordination'. Thus during normal times of relatively low class conflict, proportionally more members of the working class uncritically accept the values of literacy and education than do upper-class radicals. For most members of the working class, the acquiring of literacy and education is one way to advance in a class-based society; and opposition to school teachers and to authority from schoolchildren and unemployed teenagers represents a complaint that they have been denied an equal chance to acquire these values. It is necessary to break out of the ideology you are brought up in to be able to view society as a whole and see the historical role of literacy, as Edmund Leach does when he argues for a new type of literacy (see Document 5).

It would appear to most people that common sense has nothing whatever to do, by definition, with politics or ideology. But ideology is in fact most influential in just that area where its influence is most denied. Ideology, uncritically accepted systems of ideas, frequently prevents us from questioning those common-sense values that most closely surround us.

Your own ideologies will have a powerful influence on the decisions you will take in your project work. At first, the decisions you take, in using or rejecting sources and materials, will seem to you simply a matter of common sense. As you become more aware of the complexities of communication, however, you will also become increasingly conscious of your own ideologies and how they govern the decisions you take. Awareness of your ideologies does not render them false or 'incorrect'. It simply aids your own understanding of the process in which you are involved, with yourself as a central actor.

The ideology that literacy is a value and must, if possible, be improved is not arbitrary: it is necessary to, and in tune with, a society that is becoming technologically more sophisticated. It would be very much more difficult for somebody who disagreed with the development of such a society (somebody who advocates a pre-industrial mode of living, for example) to communicate with Alderson or Collins. Such an ideology would be out of tune with social development and might reject the existence of the mass media in its entirety *because* it rejects industrial society. Such fundamental ideological differences amount to a major problem in communication. If in the course of your project work you remain alert for such ideological elements in the material you consult, it should help you become sensitive to and isolate, even if you cannot overcome, such problems in communication. In the case of literacy, for example, you might only be able to note that such a problem exists, and to suggest an alternative definition of literacy — for example, as a means of preserving power in the hands of an educated elite.

Selection

When Alderson quotes from her opponents' statements she is making a conscious selection from their views in order to comment on them later. She may or may not be aware of the possibility that she is being biased in her selection of such extracts. Selection is practised constantly in human communication, but the communicator is not always aware of the criteria by which selections are made. The criteria for the selections — whether the communicator is aware of them or not — are the evidence for his or her *ideology*.

Since project work allows you considerable freedom in determining content, it is important that you become aware towards the beginning of your work of the implications of the process of selection and its relation to questions of ideology. Unless you become alert to these issues early on, you may become too involved with your material and less able to assess its effectiveness as a piece of communication. In striving to maintain such distance, you should become increasingly sensitive to the nature of your material, your audience and yourself. You should also become increasingly aware of the ideologies, whether implicit or explicit, of the authors you consult when working on your project.

Weiss (1968) has pointed out the political content of communication in this way:

> Every word that I write down and submit for publication is political. It is intended to make contact with a large audience and to achieve a definite effect. I turn over my writings to one of the communications media, and then they are absorbed by the consumers. The way in which my words are received depends to a great extent on the social system under which they are distributed. Since my words are but a small and ever diminishing fraction of available opinions, I have to achieve the greatest possible precision if my views are to make their way. (p. 20)

Even though the intention behind your writing may not be in any way political, you should consider the extent to which your work is governed by the factors to which Weiss refers. You are in the fortunate position in carrying out your project work of controlling to a greater extent than Weiss both the content and the media. Nevertheless, the way in which your words are received depends also on the social system under which your project will be distributed. Imagine, for example, the changes you would have to make in your project if you were presenting it to a Soviet, American or a Third-World audience. This should increase your awareness of the influence of the social system in which you live upon the communication you will produce.

Language codes

Bernstein, who introduces Alderson's book, was responsible for pioneering work on the differences between language codes. You will need to become aware of such differences in the course of your project work, since you are likely to find yourself interviewing and talking to people with different language codes from your own. These can become a barrier to communication — they are more or less certain to be if you, as a student of communication, fail to become aware of them and take such differences into account.

Bernstein (1973) was originally concerned with the language of schoolchildren. He relates the type of language used to the social class of the user, suggesting that working-class children tend to use a 'restricted', and middle-class children an 'elaborated', code. But social class is not of itself the sole factor, for such middle-class institutions as the boys' public school or the golf-club bar also establish their own restricted codes. The existence of a community allows the development of a restricted code, though we might note that the middle class have more choice as to whether or not they will use a restricted code; for the working class it seems to be socially decided.

The restricted code is simpler, carrying a smaller vocabulary and syntax than the elaborated. It tends to be oral and to use more non-verbal means. An elaborated code may be written or spoken and tends to be more appropriate for symbolic use.

There is much greater emphasis, according to Bernstein, on non-verbal communication in the restricted code, whereas the elaborate code is almost exclusively verbal. The messages of the restricted code are often highly predictable and specific, tend to lack referential functions and include a high level of redundant language; the elaborated code is usually less predictable, and it tends to express abstractions and generalities. The restricted code tends to reinforce similarities between speaker and group, while the elaborated emphasizes individuality.

You should note also that the words used to describe these two codes themselves carry social approval and disapproval in our society. As you carry through your project work, you will develop your own judgements as to which of these two codes is the more appropriate for the purposes of communication in different situations. We should note here only that the existence of such codes, though not absolutely defined, does relate to the existence of different social classes, and that the social mobility of the person who can use both codes is likely, therefore, to be much greater than that of the person confined to only one (Fiske, 1982). (Whether or not the person with the elaborated code is accepted if s/he adopts the restricted one in order to communicate with somebody who uses restricted code, is, of course, another question!)

Simply because Bernstein is commenting upon social class, he does not become free of class influences, any more than Gramsci, when commenting upon the existence of ideology, is free of his own. The primary task is to develop an awareness of the operation of such ideologies and their influence upon the process of communication.

Bias

We must next ask ourselves the question: to what extent can any observer of an event report that event to another without adding some interpretation of it in some way? The problem of bias most obviously occurs to students when dealing with political, sociological or historical aspects of a course. Historians, for example, produce their books and television programmes, not just by researching and including material but also by rejecting material they deem unimportant. If you want to get an idea of the historian's point of view, don't consider only his final text or programme; you need to look at what is in his waste-paper basket or on his cutting-room floor as well.

At a less apparent level, each communicator is a human being offering interpretations of the world through the process of perception of, and communication about, the event. 'The image of the telephone switchboard conceives of communication in purely mechanical and technological terms' (Mortensen and Schneider, 1972). But human beings, with viewpoints about the events of the real world, are in fact the switchboard operators, not computers.

Gerbner's model, introduced in chapter 3, attempts to deal with the related problems of selection, interpretation and reporting. Are we forced to conclude from it that we are all so trapped in our own points of view, are all so biased in our reporting of events in the world, that we cannot usefully use other people's secondary material in project work? Of course not: this would be as absurd a conclusion as that you cannot believe anything you read in the newspapers because on occasion newspapers can be shown to be guilty of mis-reporting!

To deal with this problem in project work you must try to identify as early as possible the *point of view* of the author whose material you are using (the very process of writing your own diary should help you become increasingly aware of your *own* point of view about your project). The following Assignment is designed to help you isolate and describe the *point of view* of an author.

ASSIGNMENT U

1. Select a newspaper feature article of at least 300 words. Summarize what you take to be the author's point of view towards the subject matter dealt with in the article.
2. Ask a colleague to do the same.
3. Compare the two summaries. (If there are differences between the summaries this possibly indicates that you and your colleague hold different points of view about the original material.)
4. Use these summaries as the basis for distinguishing between the author's point of view and the factual. elements in the original article.

DOCUMENT 28

On bias in reporting, Hayakawa (1974) has commented:

When, for example, a newspaper tells a story in a way that we dislike, leaving out facts we think important and playing up important facts in ways that we think unfair, we are tempted to say, 'Look how unfairly they've slanted the story!' In making such a statement we are, of course, making an inference about the newspaper's editors. We are assuming that what seems important or unimportant to us seems equally important or unimportant to them, and on the basis of that assumption we infer that the editors 'deliberately' gave the story a misleading emphasis. Is this necessarily the case? Can the reader, as an outsider, say whether a story assumes a given form because the editors 'deliberately slanted it that way' or because that was the way the events appeared to them?

The point is that, by the process of selection and abstraction imposed on us by our own interests and background, experience comes to all of us (including newspaper editors) already 'slanted'. If you happen to be pro-labour, pro-Catholic, and a stock-car racing fan, your ideas of what is important or unimportant will of necessity be different from those of a man who happens to be indifferent to all three of your favourite interests. If, then, newspapers often side with the big businessman on public issues, the reason is less a matter of 'deliberate' slanting than the fact that publishers are often, in enterprises as large as modern urban newspapers, big businessmen themselves, accustomed both in work and in social life to associating with other big businessmen. Nevertheless, the best newspapers, whether owned by 'big business-men' or not, do try to tell us as accurately as possible what is going on in the world, because they are run by newspapermen who conceive it to be part of their professional responsibility to present fairly the conflicting point of view in controversial issues. Such newspapermen are *reporters* indeed.

The writer who is neither an advocate nor an opponent avoids slanting, except when he is seeking special literary effects. The avoidance of slanting is not only a matter of being fair and impartial; it is even more importantly a matter of making good maps of the territory of experience. The profoundly biased individual cannot make good maps because he can see an enemy *only* as an enemy and a friend *only* as a friend. The individual with genuine skill in writing — one who has imagination and insight — can look at the same subject from many points of view. (pp. 44-5)

It is true that newspapers often side in their reporting with businessmen because the people who own the newspapers are businessmen themselves; but Hayakawa's last comment casts doubt on whether journalists are always subject to that all-pervasive sense of professional integrity to enforce fairness in reporting.

For not only can the 'individual with genuine skill in writing . . . look at the same subject from many points of view', he or she can also use this skill to write to the particular point of view of the newspaper owner who pays his or her salary. And even the best intentioned journalist, who writes an absolutely 'fair' report on an event, may well find that the story that eventually appears in print has been altered substantially. The journalist submits each story to the sub-editor, who has the job of checking it and amending it if necessary to ensure that it is written in clear, accurate English and conforms to the style of the newspaper. Sub-editors believe that they are able to improve in many cases the copy submitted by the journalist, even though they have not been involved at the story's source and will not, for example, have spoken to any of the people the journalist may have inter-viewed. In theory, the sub-editor will check with the journalist before rewriting any aspect of the story that alters its sense. But in practice, since newspapers are produced to a deadline, sub-editors frequently lack the time.

Another of the sub-editor's jobs is to condense the story so that it will fit into the planned newspaper page. Here critical phrases or even whole paragraphs, which the journalist included originally to add balance and 'fairness' to the story, can be lost. The process of alteration continues as the sub-editor sends the story to the 'stone' sub-editor, who works closely with the printer at the task of fitting the story exactly into its allotted space in the page design. There is no time left to re-write the story; it is often simply a matter of throwing away a final qualifying paragraph, thus destroying again the balan-cing 'fair' element in the original story. Decisions are taken at this final stage on technical rather than editorial grounds. It is necessary, therefore, to balance Hayakawa's notion of the skilful, fair journalist who wants to make maps of the territories of human experience, with the practical effects of the system of production of newspapers in the mass media. It is this *system*, and the ideology of the reporting journalist, that prevent a totally unbiased and 'fair' reporting of the events of the real world. Total objectivity is impossible; but it would certainly improve communication if editors and reporters laid bare to the reader the viewpoints they hold.

Project pressures

Although you are not subjected to the same economic or financial pressures and considerations as the newspaper journalist, you should consider the nature of the other pressures on you which will alter your original conception of what you were going to report into the final version which appears in your project. You might find it easier to become aware of these pressures if you take into account the following factors:

Limitations of time available.
Limitations on access to source material.
Limitations of your own ability to make use of these sources.
Original preconceptions about your subject matter.
Degree to which you are receptive to new ways of approaching this subject matter.
Personal attitudes towards people you need to interview in the course of your project work.
Degree to which you can overcome personal limitations in approaching, talking to, interviewing, people with information of use to you in your project work.
Limitations on time available for writing up the project.
Pressures of deadlines which prevent you from taking proper account of new directions and ideas in your project work.
Degree to which you are reluctant to change the structure of your project simply because it is 'easier' to carry on with the original structure.

Degree to which you are prevented from changing the structure to a more appropriate shape due to the requirements of the examining body.

Pressures produce bias

Here is a further comment about the problem of bias, made by the student who did the project on Countesthorpe College. This is the conclusion she reached after extensive research into the treatment the school received from the local press. However, she was not content to simply research into secondary sources. She went to the trouble of tracing the reporters who had written some of these stories in the local paper and interviewed them in order to probe further the question of bias. Here, particular investigation and research developed, for the student, a general hypothesis about bias in reporting, an hypothesis which can be further tested by application to later 'chunks' of communicative experience and modified as necessary.

DOCUMENT 29

It is particularly interesting to compare the above quotes of John Watts and those of the local newspaper from the same HMI report. A study of the local press reports reveals that they do give a fairly balanced report as far as facts are concerned, but the way the articles are constructed gives emphasis to the controversial aspects. Headlines for example set the tone or angle of the article, i.e the words 'disaster' and 'suffering when things go wrong' in a headline implies 'failure', when the substantial facts within the article may suggest otherwise. Therefore it is the technique and treatment of the college reports which is questionable — more often than the content. However, there are some articles which simply highlight the controversial history and failures of the college, completely disregarding any advancements and improvements. For example, one article printed in the *Leicester Mercury* in June 1974 was headed 'The history: threats, abuse and vandalism'. This contained a very depressing account of the college's history with selected facts and occurrences, although the facts were true.

It is interesting to compare the headlines of a national newspaper to those of the local newspaper, reporting on the same issue:

The Guardian 'Parents support school staff'
The *Leicester Mercury* 'College warden admits errors were made'

Articles written by Virginia Makins, deputy editor of the *Times Educational Supplement*, also contrast with those of the *Leicester Mercury*. Ms Makins visited the school regularly since it opened and has taken her evidence from parents and people involved with the educational system locally, nationally and internationally. The whole tone of her writing is different. Strikingly, there is an absence of the sensationalism which the *Mercury* has been criticized for. The articles are unbiased and give equal weight to improvements and the importance of the college, as it does to the setbacks.

This evidence proves that the interpretation of news material depends to a large extent on your own point of view. When reading articles we do not believe everything we read, but we accept the evidence which is compatible with our attitudes and beliefs. Perhaps subconsciously, we reject news reports which contain ideas which we do not agree with.

The truth of this is indicated powerfully, in this case, by the fact that 'if a school is not a bad school, and most importantly has the confidence of the parents, bad publicity cannot damage the school and may even strengthen it by bringing in the parents' (Mack, 1978). In the particular case of Countesthorpe College, parents dominated a public meeting with a 'bitter, vehement and prolonged attack on the *Leicester Mercury*'s correspondent who was present about what they considered to be the *Mercury*'s blatantly unfair coverage. The parents had first-hand experience of the school. . . . . Reading second-hand accounts cannot change views that are based on experience.' In this case, the professional gatekeeper was exposed directly to criticism from a minority of the paper's audience, an audience whose passivity is generally largely taken for granted. You should, of course, try to avoid the consequences of any similar complacency as you develop special expertise in your own particular field of project work.

An understanding of ideology, selection, language codes and bias should help you to become aware of your own power as originator and author of your project. You will become the gatekeeper.

Skills

Design, interviewing, and the organization of feedback, are three skills you will need to master if you are going to apply the above concepts successfully. There is a close connection between concepts and skills in project work. For example, you cannot become a skilful interviewer if you have not developed an awareness of ideology and language codes. We shall cover here only a limited number of the skills necessary in project work, both because of limitations of space and because it is better to illustrate thoroughly, with examples, the nature of some central skills than merely to list a large number.

Design

Our culture tends to emphasize that meaning (and hence ideology, bias and viewpoint) exists in *words* rather than in non-verbal symbols. When designing any necessary *illustrations* for your project, you are thus less likely to be aware of such issues than when dealing with more explicit verbal meanings. We tend to regard questions of illustration and design as being relatively value free.

Figure 16 is the title page from the student's project on Countesthorpe College. It carries with it its own set of assumptions about the characteristics of its audience. This front-cover design (originally A4 size), while well balanced and executed, fails to achieve fully the intended effect, since it assumes too great a familiarity with the subject on the part of the audience. The significance of the elaboration of the letter 'C' in 'Countesthorpe College', while attractive in itself, is lost on the majority of the audience. The design of this letter is an attempt to indicate what the college buildings look like from an aerial view. An aerial photograph (figure 17) is later included in the body of the project, but for most of the parents reading the project the front-cover design carries little

significance, particularly at first sight, when presumably it is intended to have maximum impact. The author has transferred some of *her* viewpoint and familiarity with her subject matter to her audience—a temptation which occurs regularly in project work as you familiarize yourself increasingly with your material, and which must be just as regularly resisted.

Images and meaning

The more a society relies on words to convey meaning, the less conscious its people tend to be of non-verbal symbols. This does not mean that we do not use them extensively. But it might mean that you, brought up in such a society, will place relatively little emphasis on the design aspects and too much on the purely verbal aspects of your communication. This tendency will almost certainly have been reinforced by your schooling, for our education system also tends to over-value the written word and to undervalue other types of sign. Fiske (1982) gives detailed consideration to the ways that visual images signify and to the role that words play in directing our reading of them. Dyer (1982) also suggests some interesting ways of analysing the visual content of advertisements in order to reach an understanding of how they mean what they do.

Consider again the leisure facilities' case study of chapter 2. How comfortable would we have been with an exhibition of photographs in the local library which contained no captions at all? And yet surely we would agree that the 'message' of the exhibition is conveyed primarily by the photographs rather than the captions. Although we all use non-verbal signals in our society extensively, there has been far less

OUNTESTHORPE OLLEGE

An Introduction and A Defence

by A Current Student

Figure 16

Figure 17

research into the implications of these than there has been into written meanings. Similarly, although most people are far more capable and comfortable when they are communicating orally rather than in writing, and although this is the predominant medium of communication for the majority of people in our society, most of the time, relatively little time is spent in our educational institutions improving oral communication in comparison with the amount of time spent improving written communication (see, for example, Document 5).

Since we are surrounded by images, and since we tend not to subject them to extensive criticism in our educational system, we tend to swim uncritically in the environment created by them. Of course, we all know from school classes on the media that advertising can be a 'bad influence' on us because advertisements attempt to sell us things, but the analysis rarely goes beyond that. But, as Berger (1972) (Document 30) points out, when writing of the 'publicity image':

DOCUMENT 30

In the cities in which we live, all of us see hundreds of publicity images every day of our lives. No other kind of image confronts us so frequently.

In no other form of society in history has there been such a concentration of images, such a density of visual messages.

One may remember or forget these messages but briefly one takes them in, and for a moment they stimulate the imagination by way of either memory or expectation. The publicity image belongs to the moment. We see it as we turn a page, as we turn a corner, as a vehicle passes us. Or we see it on a television screen whilst waiting for the commercial break to end. Publicity images also belong to the moment in the sense that they must be continually renewed and made up to date. Yet they never speak of the present. Often they refer to the past and always they speak of the future.

We are now so accustomed to being addressed by these images that we scarcely notice their total impact. A person may notice a particular image or piece of information because it corresponds to some particular interest he has. But we accept the total system of publicity images as we accept an element of climate. For example, the fact that these images belong to the moment but speak of the future produces a strange effect which has become so familiar that we scarcely notice it. Usually it is *we* who pass the image — walking, travelling, turning a page; on the TV screen it is somewhat different but even then we are theoretically the active agent —we can look away, turn down the sound, make some coffee. Yet, despite this, one has the impression that publicity images are continually passing us, like express trains on their way to some distant terminus. We are static; they are dynamic—until the newspaper is thrown away, the television programme continues or the poster is posted over. (p. 129)

Here, Berger uses the term 'publicity image' to include 'advertising image'. You should attempt to bear his comments constantly in mind as you encounter problems of design in project work — for he is drawing attention to the way in which viewpoint and ideology influence supposedly neutral and value-free graphic communication.

When Berger analyses the 'time-status' of the publicity image he deals with the *ideology* that is implicit in the use of such images in our society. They are, he suggests, intended to create a dissatisfaction in people.

Publicity images have a strange effect in that they become so familiar that we hardly notice them; they have become, apparently, visual common sense. For most people, they become simply an accepted part of looking at the world.

Berger goes on to point out that in our society most people tend to assume, since there are many different publicity images, that they do in fact compete with each other since they are used to promote different products. In reality, however, each publicity image tends to confirm and enhance every other.

> Publicity is not merely an assembly of competing messages, it is a language in itself which is always being used to make the same general proposal. Within publicity choices are offered between this cream and that cream, that car and this car, but publicity as a system only makes a single proposal. It proposes to each of us that we transform ourselves, or our lives, by buying something more. This more, it proposes, will make us in some way richer—even though we will be poorer by having spent our money. (p. 130)

Thus the ideology that it is a good idea for each individual to become as rich in possessions as possible becomes the prevailing common-sense agreement in our society. The image is conveyed in a visual language that itself tends to obscure the *content* of publicity.

The criteria for appropriate design are the same as the criteria for effective written communication. You should therefore ask yourself the same questions of any design work you need to include in your project as you do of written communication. The comments upon the publicity image and on ideology in graphic communication are intended to increase your *awareness* of the operation of these factors since, typically, you will not have been encouraged to develop a sensitivity to them. Berger's is an extreme example, perhaps, but then you should constantly be on the look out for the operation of ideology and viewpoint in such graphic communication.

Interviewing

The next part of this chapter deals in more detail with the skill of interviewing—a skill you will need to develop as fully as possible if you are to get the maximum from project material. Projects cannot be confined to secondary sources — books, newspapers, periodicals, etc.; you must also go to those primary sources —people — on which those secondary sources are themselves originally based. You have the opportunity here to accumulate, organize and present such primary material; to interview, for example, people who have never before been interviewed about their involvement in a particular aspect of life, perhaps because nobody has hitherto regarded their views as interesting. You may find youself involved in such 'living history' in project work.

Here's one example (Document 31), taken from interviews about work in the cotton factories in Bristol at about the time of the First World War:

DOCUMENT 31

The Great Western Cotton Factory in Barton Hill was completed in 1838. By 1840 it was employing 1040 people. The two largest buildings were the five-storey spinning block and the single-storey weaving shed. A working man wrote of conditions for the operatives in the 1880s in the following terms:

Young girls leave their homes soon after 5 o'clock in the morning — some who have come from long distances even earlier than this — to trudge through all kinds of weather, winter and summer, to get to the factory at 6 a.m. and if they arrive two minutes late, they have a fine inflicted on them out of all proportion to the rate of wages they are paid. We will follow one into the factory. She goes into the weaving shed, and as the day goes on we find she is working in a temperature of 100 degrees and in a damp atmosphere that makes her clothes soaking wet. Look, there stands the girl at her loom, with her apron to her eyes, wiping away the tears which she cannot repress. Listen and you will hear her say, 'I would rather the workhouse or gaol than this'. That is no fiction of the mind but cruel fact, and far from a solitary one.

In 1889 the operatives came out for a reduction in hours (to start at 8 instead of 6 and to finish at 5.30), and a 10 per cent increase in wages. Processions and mass meetings were arranged. After a month-long strike the employers conceded everything except the increase in wages.

Many still remember the cotton workers' clogs and shawls and many more remember the imposing factory buildings situated on the feeder canal at Barton Hill. In 1925 the factory was transformed into an artificial silk mill. By 1929 the work at the mill stopped and the reconstructed machinery was smashed. The main part of the factory was demolished in 1968, but some of the people who worked there are still alive. Mrs Melhuish is one of them and she is one of the first people that we interviewed.

[In the introduction to these interviews the following comment is made: 'If people see themselves as taking an active part in history, then it makes the task of organizing for a better society that much easier.']

Mrs Melhuish: I started work at the cotton factory when I was fourteen and I started in the weaving shed at first. Wages to commence with were 3/7d per week. Out of 3/7d per week I had to pay 3d for a pocket that you put round your waist. . . . Anyway, I was only there for a few days, that was before Christmas. I thought I was doing well. I was told I was doing alright. So the woman in charge said she was going down to the pub to have a drink, she wouldn't be very long, could I go on with the job. So I said 'Yes, to the best of my ability I will.' (If you remember, I'm only 14.) So away she goes to the pub and away I gets on with the machine.

When she comes back she finds this long streak down the calico. 'Oh,' she says, 'what's that, how long has that been going on?'

I said, 'For some time, what's the trouble?'

She said, 'That's bad work, I don't get paid for none of that. All that's got to be taken off and reweaved.'

So I said 'I'm awfully sorry,' I apologized to her. I said, 'I thought I was doing my best.'

When all's said, she got into a temper, slapped my face and left her fingermarks on my face. So I thought, well the only thing I can do now is give her one back, So I picked up the bobbin and let her have one back, see.

So the foreman says, 'What's going on here?'

So I said, 'Well she slapped me across the face, you can still see the marks. I got into a bit of a paddy and hit her one with this bobbin.'

So he said, 'That's enough of that then. You go to the office and get your cards. You're finished.'

I said, 'I can't tell my mother and father that I've got the sack. It wasn't actually my fault.'

He said 'Never mind, get your cards and out you go.'

The extract presents hitherto hidden detail which has been revealed by questions to Mrs Melhuish. It conveys a condensed significance of detail that would not normally be achieved in interviews without you, the interviewer, carefully preparing the questions and using discriminatingly the answers that are given.

As you interview, and after you have interviewed, you should reflect on the *process* of communication that took place between you as interviewer and your interviewees.

In this next extract (Document 32) some students (S) working on a project on housing in different areas of Leeds, are themselves being interviewed by their tutors (*MG* and *MB*) about their experiences and what they have learned from those experiences.

The students' interviews with residents at Quarry Hills had produced some unreliable and conflicting facts and figures, so they had gone to Leeds council housing offices for official, more reliable information.

DOCUMENT 32

MG Did you work out an interview system . . . or did you just evolve it as you went along?

S Well, it depends. You go from one area to another and the people are completely different. They've got — you know — in one area, say, you get people who are tenants of the council and have been fighting the council for years — about their rent — and they don't really want to talk about the rent because it kind of brings, you know, back, some of the ideas, and they don't like being on tape saying things about the people. . . . Or you get a really happy situation with a family . . . this man with absolutely hundreds of kids, absolutely hundreds, you know, and that sort of person you can talk about anything to, because they've always got their wife, and she's sweating over the sink — you know and it gets him going. You mostly find that, that the men want to be more serious and the women don't. The women like to . . .

MG Well I'd think some of the women might just be rather pleased to have a chat . . .

S Yeah, we met a woman in a Leeds house, she had thousands of cats, she showed us round the whole flat, let us take photographs . . . it's quite a demand on people, immediately they see cameras they think 'Oh —'

I was surprised actually that it wasn't the other way round — that they'd rather not — but they weren't bothered one bit about tapes. Ninety per cent of people aren't bothered at all by tapes. We didn't have any trouble at all except with the council. You just stick it up — they rather like it because it's like Radio Leeds . . . But the council, you know what they do? They send you to one place. 'Oh we can answer you one question, yes' they say. 'How many houses are there in — ?' 'Well, I think there's 150, but there again there might be 600. Or there again there might be 10,000! I think you'd better go up to . . .' And they send you all the way up to somewhere or other. You know, they send you to —. You must go and see this one individual — they send you all over the place, you know, it's the way they do it. They, they never say 'We can't tell you that' — unless you ask a controversial question and they just fob it off — but if you want statistical information you have to really construct it . . . they send you to another place.

MB   It'd certainly test your powers of persuasion . . .

S   They know the pattern. I mean, I'll show you. They've even got a room for—to give you information—you've got to the door, and you say 'I'm a student' and they say here you are [shows piles of printed leaflets] — I mean it's absolutely — it, it gives you how many flats there are, but it's not like a tape. I mean, if you go into an exhibition and you see something on the wall — four pages foolscap of statistics — you'd never read them I mean, I wouldn't. Well if you have piles of typed out things like this . . . no one's going to read it . . . and they keep referring to it, they keep saying — you say 'And how many people didn't want to live in flats?' and they say 'Oh but it's all in that leaflet you've got.' What they're frightened of is the question you're going to ask after that — if you're going to ask a controversial question. . . . And if you ask a controversial question they'll answer it so quickly that you can't write it down. They're very clever. Not clever — just used to it . . .

MG   Do you feel you've now got enough data from your interviews?

S   Yes.

MB   It's the evaluation of it now which is quite important.

S   Yeah, it's probably the most difficult thing. It's too easy going around asking questions. It's *editing*, the actual writing it up. Just to make one tape of you saying something for an hour and a half, you've got to write it all out for a start. That's the worst. We've first of all got to decide what to use. You get the information at the start, and it doesn't really matter, the more the merrier. You try and keep along certain lines, within bounds but it doesn't really matter if you go outside your bounds . . . you have a basic idea for your project but you can expand on it.

Five months later the students reflected on what they had learned about interviewing for project work and how they had learned it. These reflections are included in question 3 of the following Assignment (V).

ASSIGNMENT V

1. Compare the speech patterns used in the two extracts above (Documents 31 and 32) with those from the punctuated speech of Maurice Plaskow (which appears at the beginning of chapter 1). Attempt to account for the differences in the light of Bernstein's distinctions between restricted and elaborated speech codes described earlier in this chapter.
2. Write a summary of the principles for effective interviewing that you believe the students have learned.
3. The following extract represents the students' own reflections on the learning that took place five months after the interviewing.

MB   Did you learn much about your topic of housing from the interview method?

S   We learned firsthand, we got firsthand information about housing. We found that this was the best method of get, of getting information. It's no real use in writing letters to, to Council officials 'cos you get a kind of official letter back — a kind of letter almost off a banda machine. The best thing to do is to go and actually see someone, sit on their doorstep until they answer the questions or, or you get your information. The best way of getting information for a subject like this is by the interview method, by direct contact with those who are involved directly with what you're trying to learn about or find out about.

MB   Did you learn to communicate more effectively yourself?

S   Yes, you learn to assess a situation in terms of communication. That's what you learn from interviewing. You learn that what you're getting from the person has got to be moulded into an end result. Interviewing isn't a chit-chatty thing, it's a formal way of extracting information.

Compare your summary of what the students learned with the students' own reflections. Try to account for any differences in brevity, depth and perspective.

Purpose in interview work

An essential element in getting Mrs Melhuish to talk so freely and significantly was sympathy on the part of the interviewer. Allied to this, however, must be competence in technique and a sensitivity to the purpose of the interview. If, for example, you want to interview your subject *only* about her views on work in the early years of this century, you will have to ensure that your interjections or supplementary questions bring your interviewee back to that subject; *or* that your later write-up of the interview edits out irrelevant material. You have to balance sympathy with your subject and interviewee against the purpose of the interview.

You might find it useful to put yourself in the position of somebody being interviewed in order to frame the most useful questions and approach to the interview. MacShane (1979), for example, considers different purposes that a trade unionist might have in mind when being interviewed during a hospital strike. They may vary from wanting to get his side of the story across in the face of slanted press coverage, through a desire to inspire sympathetic action by union members elsewhere, to wanting to enhance the image of his union. Try to work out before you commence the interview what is likely to be the main purpose of the person being interviewed and assess to what extent it coincides with your own.

Is the interviewee keen to help you get the specific information you require, or simply glad of the opportunity to talk to someone? When framing your questions you should leave the fewest possible number of variables so that the interviewee will produce answers easily assimilable by your audience. In the case of the trade unionists, the audience may be members of the union not involved in the particular issue; or trade unionists and active supporters; or the public at large; or other employers to whom the unionist intends to deliver a warning; or the particular hospital management with whom he is in dispute.

Feedback

One method of assessing the progress of a project is by testing elements of it on selected samples of the audience. (If this is impossible then, as I mentioned earlier, your tutor or members of your class may serve as a substitute.) Results from this testing might lead to modifications of part of the project. Such testing should also provide you with guidelines as to the best method of obtaining the feedback you will need when your project is completed.

The concept of feedback distinguishes work in communication studies, where it is essential, from work in English literature, where it is incidental. The concept is to be found in both the biological and physical sciences. Much of the pioneering work in developing the concept was done by Wiener who, working with Rosenblueth, introduced the term 'cybernetics':

> The simplest feedback systems with which most people are familiar are the Watt steam governor, which regulates the speed of a steam engine, and the thermostat, which controls the temperature of a room. The needs of the war forced attention to feedback systems with the urgency of developing automatic predictors, automatic gun-laying mechanisms, and many other automatic following, 'self-controlling', or 'goal-seeking', systems. Wiener and Rosenblueth called attention to the need for a general study that would cover not only these automatic mechanisms but also certain aspects of physiology, the central nervous sytem, and the operation of the brain, and even certain problems in economics concerning the theory of booms and slumps. The common thread linking these topics, whether mechanical, biological or electrical, is the idea of communication of information and the setting up of self-stabilizing control action. (Cherry, 1957, p. 57)

You should attempt at an early stage to establish fairly precisely the level of understanding and information held about the subject or your project topic by your audience. This can be done by testing a sample audience before fully exposing your project work.

When drawing up your questionnaire (or other form of feedback) you may also find it useful to consult material on the social composition of modern Britain so that you can relate your specific findings to the general social situation. How representative of the population in general are the particular conclusions you are drawing from your sample?

Let's attempt to illustrate how to obtain feedback from the audience for a project by looking at a particular example. The following questionnaire (Document 33) was devised to assess the effectiveness of a written and illustrated project, 'A maintenance guide for a Morris Minor 1000'.

Comment

The student's explanatory note on the questionnaire ran:

> This information was collected to find out whether the basic maintenance guide 'Morris Minor 1000' had successfully met the aims it purported to.
>
> A number of audience members had a minimum of two hours to examine the contents of the guide and to answer the ten questions shown.
>
> The Morris Minor owner-drivers were residents of the Thurnby Lodge and Scraptoft districts of Leicester and were varied in age and sex; a cross-section of opinion is thus represented.

Where your sample is more extensive than the one above, it is useful to go into more detail about its composition, so that the examiners can get a thorough idea of the basis of the conclusions you are drawing from your feedback.

Here your interviewing is for a purpose other than primary research for project material, but the criteria for successful interviewing detailed above should again be applied. In particular, when interviewing to obtain feedback you should resist the temptation to try to find out too much from the people you are going to interview. Nothing is more likely to prevent a fruitful response from an interviewee than the sight of an interviewer armed with a long list of questions that could take two hours or so to answer! Remember that your project is of much greater importance to you than it is to the interviewee, whose encounter with the subject may in fact be fairly brief. Don't transfer your assumptions to your audience.

It is worth taking particular note of special cases amongst the respondents—those audience members who fail to reply in the way that you expect them to. This may give you a general clue as to the nature of the problem: does it lie with (a) you as a communicator; (b) the nature of the project material itself; (c) the particular sampling technique employed; (d) the nature of this particular member of the audience—was he/she significantly different from your average audience member?

The main temptation you must avoid is to devise your questionnaire so that it will produce only the specific results that you want. An extreme example of such unscientific construction of a questionnaire was noticed by the *New Statesman* (27 October 1978) when it investigated the way in which the London *Evening News* carried out its survey of the standards of education in London primary schools. The *New Statesman* established that the whole of the survey was to be carried out by freelance contributors. A letter to these journalists from the *Evening News'* news editor asked them to 'please arrange to interview ten children from as many schools as possible aged ten years or over who are still attending primary school. They should come from as wide a range of schools as possible. We would like each of them to answer the following six questions (you may find some children will

DOCUMENT 33

Age _____

Sex _____

<u>Feedback Questionnaire</u>

1. Have you had any previous experience in motor-vehicle maintenance?
   ☐ A fair amount ☐ Very little ☐ None

2. If you have had very little or no previous experience, after reading the guide, how interested would you be in taking up your own basic motor-vehicle maintenance?
   ☐ Not at all interested ☐ Fairly interested
   ☐ Very interested

3. Did you find that humour in the guide helped to communicate the actual contents?
   ☐ Yes ☐ No

4. Did you think that the level of work being asked to carry out was
   ☐ Too high ☐ Correct ☐ Too low

5. Did the guide help you gain a better appreciation of your car?
   ☐ Yes ☐ No

6. Would you use the guide to trace and rectify simple faults that might occur on your car?
   ☐ Yes ☐ No

7. Is there any information in the guide which you thought was unnecessary?

8. Is there any information that you thought should have been added?

9. Do you think that the cover would attract your attention if placed in a public place such as a refectory or library?
   ☐ Yes ☐ No

10. Are there any further criticisms or comments you would like to make about the guide? (Continue overleaf if you need to.)

give the wrong answers for fun. Please be on the alert for these and disregard them accordingly).' The journalists were told to accept only a more-or-less immediate answer and not to wait for children to count up laboriously on their fingers. The *New Statesman* commented:

> Apart from the stupidity of relying on six questions to judge entire standards in primary education, the survey appears to suggest that the intelligence of the journalists involved must seriously be questioned. Do they not know that any firm needing reliable information would not dream of conducting research in such an arbitrary way? Are they not aware that teaching methods in primary schools have changed a little since the days they were asked to recite tables in a classroom? Since no survey has yet appeared — the rival *Evening Standard* [these two papers have since been amalgamated] produced its own feature based on interviews with people involved with the profession — perhaps the *Evening News* has thought better of it.

This incident raises the question of the purpose behind the survey; if the newspaper genuinely wanted to discover what the standards in education were, then it would have devised a much more scientifically-based survey, which would have attempted to poll a cross-section of children by social class and insisted on regional balance. If, however, it wanted to make a political point, then the survey it had devised would probably have done the job.

Guidelines for questionnaires

As guidelines for the construction of a questionnaire you should remember to:

Start with an attitude of 'not knowing'

Conduct your survey genuinely in order to learn — not to prove!

Jettison any preconceived ideas you may have about results.

Attempt to be absolutely accurate in the conducting of your survey.

Use a scientifically accurate sample.

Avoid using excessively complicated questions.

Point out clearly in a note any weaknesses or limitations in your method.

Interviewing: a model

The process of interpersonal communication that takes place during interviews, and the obtaining of feedback, has been described diagrammatically by Ross (1965). When doing project work in these areas you should attempt to take as much account as possible of the factors included in his model (figure 18).

ASSIGNMENT W

Consider the application of Ross's model of interpersonal communication to the discussion of their interviewing experiences by the students working on the project 'Housing in Leeds' (Document 32, Assignment V).

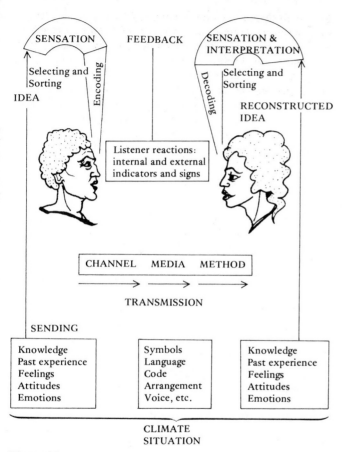

Figure 18

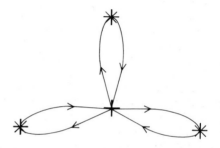

Group work on projects

Within different groups different problems of communication will arise and it is worth noting here some of the more common ones.

In a group of four, if one member tends to emerge and exercise a 'leadership function' the relationship might be represented as in figure 19.

Figure 19

Note + is the originator of particular items of information;
* a member of the group

During most presentations of project work — where the student is simply delivering the project to the audience, and *before* audience response is asked for — the situation can be represented as in figure 20.

In figure 19, much may come to depend upon an emerging leader of the group (+). He or she may produce an inhibiting effect upon other members of the group who will consequently fail to contribute what they potentially could to the project work. Discussion might be controlled too tightly by the

149

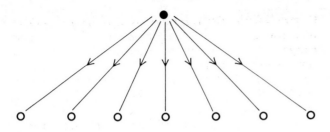

Figure 20

(*Note* ● is the student; ○ an audience member)

'leader' and useful ideas from other members neglected. There are alternative structures which can prevent the emergence of such 'leaders' and allow each group member the chance to put a point directly to the others as necessary. Disagreements about the direction of the project work, and specific plans for action can be registered rapidly and measures taken to resolve such disagreements.

Where the group structure is one of genuine equality without a 'leader', however, fruitful ideas may be generated very rapidly but be lost because nobody is recording them as they arise. Such recording is the basis for their later fuller discussion by the group. It is thus important that one member be assigned, preferably on a rotating basis, to carry out this secretarial function; and that provision is made at the end of such discussion sessions for the summing up of the useful main points that have emerged.

While establishing formal networks of communication in planning project work, you should not neglect informal

sources of many ideas. Ideas will often develop outside formal meetings; for example, two members of the group may have a particularly close relationship which may lead to the production of useful ideas, possibly even during casual conversation on distantly related topics. You should make provision for recording such ideas and for discussing them later in the group, along, of course, with ideas which occur to individuals about the course of the project.

In a group that refuses to allow a 'leader' to emerge, the situation could be represented as in figure 21.

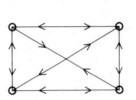 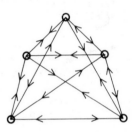

Where there are four members in the group

Where there are five members in the group

Figure 21

If you are to keep your group working effectively on your agreed project topic you will need to devise structures at an early stage to prevent undesirable divisions. A group of four might otherwise solidify into two against two; while a group of three may become two against one, with the isolated individual feeling that the attitudes of the other two towards each other and towards him make it difficult for him/her to contribute fully to the project work. An awareness that such problems may occur in group project work is perhaps the best insurance that they will not in practice arise.

If your group is larger than three, then steps will also have to be taken to ensure that at each stage of the work each member is fully informed about what is going on. It is necessary for one member of the group — again preferably in rotation — to take on the role of provider of such information. If such jobs rotate, the possibility of bureaucratic functions developing into 'leadership' can be checked; and each member of the group will get the opportunity to develop the necessary secretarial skills.

Networks of communication such as these are fundamentally informal in nature in the sense that the groups involved are invariably small and most students who find themselves working on a common project will have known each other previously. This makes it even more important that formal structures are established from an early stage, even in a small group.

Thinking about practice again

We now need to classify within our developing understanding of communication the skills, concepts and models that we have covered in chapters 5, 6 and 7. Referring back to the chart in chapter 4 (p. 86), we should attempt to identify our progress by making a note in the relevant boxes. We might, for example, begin to fill in box G thus:

> *Communication skills acquired whilst doing project work*
> Interviewing
> Design
> Obtaining of feedback, etc.

Box H:

> *Communication concepts relevant to project work*
> Selection
> Bias
> Viewpoint
> Ideology
> Language codes, etc.

Box I:

> *Communication models relevant to project work*
> Ross's model of interpersonal communication, etc.

Figure 22

You should similarly complete the relevant boxes when working through the following chapter.

This should help you to establish something approaching a 'theoretical map' of the field of communication, a territory you have begun to explore by way of our *particular* examples of case-study and project material.

ORAL WORK IN PROJECTS

8

Types

Many courses that involve project work now include an assessment of the students' oral ability to present and answer questions about their projects. In some cases the total marks given for the oral assessment will amount to one half of those allotted to the project. Alternatively, or additionally, your project may itself contain an element of oral presentation.

Live oral presentations

If you are to give a live oral presentation your talk should be thoroughly prepared and scripted. Even though you may not intend to read from a script, you should write one and have it by you when presenting your talk. You should thoroughly familiarize yourself with the script, even to the extent of learning passages from it by heart. It is a good idea to have noted under well-spaced headings on a separate piece of paper the main points your speech will cover. Alternatively you can print these on separate cards and turn them over as you work through your main points.

The advantage of these methods is that you will not feel the need to glue your eyes to your script. If you do, you will find it very difficult to make eye contact, and hence establish a relationship with your audience. There is no reason why in a live presentation you should not read particular passages of your talk from a script. This lends an air of authority to the content of your message, and also adds variety to the presentation. Your notes should not, however, be placed in such a prominent position that they prevent you from making and keeping close contact with the audience.

It is also a good idea to have rehearsed your introduction — but not to the extent that you deliver it mechanically — so that you can establish your relationship with the audience and get well into your talk before you have to refer to your notes.

Consider the general points made in this book about non-verbal communication: are there any uses of body language which will distract your audience's attention from your message?

If you are going to use humour, it is better to include it only when you have established a definite relationship with the audience; do not attempt to use humour, or visual aids, as a substitute for that relationship.

When speaking to your audience, try to maintain eye contact with as many members of the audience as possible, though without shifting your eyes too suddenly and frequently; this can suggest neurosis!

Time yourself — if you are not used to this formal method of communication, the novelty of the experience will make it very difficult for you to judge time accurately while you are speaking. Nervousness — an essential ingredient for the successful delivery of your speech — may well prevent you from remembering to look regularly at the watch on your wrist. The best plan is to place a watch near to your notes. Often, you may be surprised at 'how time flies'. This is probably due to your deep involvement in the process — really you will have been enjoying yourself although you may have felt very nervous at the outset. You should not, however, make the mistake of assuming that your audience, too, will be similarly entranced. You must constantly remain sensitive to their reactions to you and to what you are saying. Meanings are in people, not exclusively in words.

Other oral presentations

The following considerations apply to live presentations *and* to those on tape, film or video soundtracks, tape/slide sequences, etc.

If you have the opportunity before your presentation starts, arrange the room so that the seating conditions provide the best possible environment, taking account of the need for adequate ventilation and lighting.

In your delivery you should vary the tone and pitch of your voice, though you should never sacrifice clarity to such variety. A reasonable average speaking speed, suitable for most audiences, is about 150–80 words per minute. You should aim to keep your sentences short, building them into a total picture of your meaning. Do not hang subordinate clause upon main clause as additional points occur to you while you are speaking; leave such issues until later to illustrate your main points, and use shortish, separate sentences when making them.

It is essential at the outset to establish a structure for your talk; *saying what you are going to say, saying it, and finally saying what you have said*. You should not, however, allow this structure to impose a monotonous tone upon your talk. In the case of recorded talks, you have the advantage of being able to polish and edit your words, but the disadvantage of not being in contact with your audience. This can cause major problems, since it denies you the feedback needed to suit content and delivery to the needs of your audience: thus the necessity for prior research to establish their needs and the style of your oral presentation is that much greater.

Oral assessments

In addition to any oral content in the project itself, many courses in communication require the student to take part in a discussion of the project. The performance of the student in this oral is then assessed by a tutor and/or moderator and gives part of the overall mark for the project.

Gallwey (1975) has suggested that a form of 'concentrated relaxation' or 'relaxed concentration' is the most productive attitude with which to approach and perform such oral tasks. Writing from the viewpoint of a professional tennis coach, and drawing examples therefore from tennis, Gallwey argues that the causes of 'freak-outs', which impair or ruin performance, can be grouped into three categories: regret about past events, fear or uncertainty about the future, and dislike of a present event or situation. In all cases, he says, the event and the mind's reaction to it, are two separate things. It takes both to produce the result, but the 'freak-out' is in, and of, the mind; it is not an attribute of the event itself.

In the first case, argues Gallwey, the mind neglects present action and usually also becomes involved in harsh self-criticism.

In your oral examination this might occur in the following way: when dealing with the second question from the examiners, you worry instead about what you feel was a poor answer to the first question you were asked. Alternatively, your entire approach to the oral, even before you have been asked that first question, is affected adversely by your memories of a previous poor performance in an oral. This attitude prevents you from seeing things as they really are and wastes valuable energy which is better devoted to dealing, to the best of your *present* ability, with the situation you are actually in.

Secondly, you may find youself worrying about the later stages of the oral while you are still in the early stages. You have convinced yourself, for example, that things can't possibly be going as well as you feel they are and that you are bound to be confronted later with a particularly awkward question about your project which will stump you. If this mental process starts, you should attempt to stop it as soon as you realize that it is happening. You should try to bring your attention back to the 'here and now' and deal with the question being put to you with as much relaxed concentration as possible.

If it is necessary to do this, it can be valuable to focus your attention upon your own breathing—this automatically keeps you in the present rather than in the future or the past.

Gallwey argues that if we keep our minds in the present and refuse to take fear trips into the future we will find that 'there is an automatic process which gives us the necessary resources to deal with the situation at hand. As the mind learns to remain calm in critical moments it becomes able to distinguish easily between real and imagined danger.'

Thirdly, you may be inclined to 'freak out' during your oral examination due to the dislike of the situation you are in, rather than any anxiety about the past or future. Gallwey argues that there are only two possible approaches to dealing with upsetting circumstances in the present. One is to change the circumstance; the other is to change the mind which is experiencing the upset: 'he can choose to see the disturbance as stemming from his mind and not the event. Then he can find a solution. ... There are always going to be thoughts and events that try to pull our attention away from the here and now. Each is an opportunity to practise the all-important art of concentration.'

Since you are undergoing a public oral examination as part of your course in communication, you do not, in reality, have the power to change the circumstances. What you do have the power to change, however, is your attitude towards the examination. If you believe that such examinations (or even all examinations) are not a fair test of your abilities, then you have, in our society, various opportunities, though limited, to argue for a change in the system. Channels available are your school/college council academic board, the National Union of School Students, National Union of Students, and so on. But you have to recognize, equally, that an oral examination is not the place to express your attitude towards such examinations, or to argue your case for changes.

It might be useful, faced with circumstances you intensely dislike, to ask yourself why you are following your communications course. Are you following it simply in order to obtain another qualification, or are you following it in order to genuinely further your understanding of communication? If the former, then the examination is a barrier over which you are likely to feel that you have to leap; you should ask yourself, however, whether and why you really want to be qualified to follow further courses or to obtain jobs in a field which may not seriously interest you.

If you *are* genuinely interested in developing your understanding of the subject, you should approach the examination as an opportunity to do this. There will probably be many occasions in your life when you will face such interviews; try to treat the exam as an imperfect, though useful, assessment of your developing understanding of communication, and as useful preparatory experience for future interviews.

As I indicated earlier, however, you don't have to rely solely on 'inner calm'. The advice above on rehearsing what you are going to say should be read as the essential equivalent of practice on the tennis court—only don't expect to perform in the real thing exactly as you do in practice!

You should practice for your oral examination by trying to work out in advance some of the questions you are likely to be asked; put yourself in the position of your tutor/examiner in order to imagine how they might react to your project work. (You will have had some practice in such imagining when performing certain roles during case-study work.) It is a useful practice when faced with any communication task, and has benefits too in domestic, social and industrial life, in helping to isolate genuine conflicts based upon different interests, from those which arise from failures in communication or understanding of the other person's point of view. It is also valuable to consider how you would advise another student setting out in the same area of project work, somebody later attempting to achieve the same objectives for the same audience as you.

If there will be more than one assessor of your work, you should try to take into account any likely differences in their attitudes. In comparison with your tutor, for example, an external examiner may know very little about your work, and you may well need, therefore, to offer the external examiner more information than your own tutor, who will share a basic familiarity with your work.

You should also ask yourself what the primary purpose of the people interviewing you will be. Do they simply want to obtain further information from you about your project, or are they mainly interested in seeing how you evaluate the effectiveness of your project, and seeing what it has helped you to learn about communication practices, principles and models? In no way is it helpful for you to assume that their purpose in asking you the questions is simply to trip you up!

You should work out in advance how you are going to respond when points are raised in the interview which you have simply never before considered. (If you really do not understand the question put, then do not be too embarrassed to say so. Ask for it to be repeated, or expanded if necessary. It is better to respond thus than to attempt to waffle an answer to a question you have not in fact been asked.) A pause for thought is far preferable to the snap superficial answer that comes straight from the top of your head with no consideration of the complexities involved. If, at the end of this pause, you still feel that you can offer no fruitful response, it is better to admit this than to attempt a fundamentally evasive answer which is merely likely to discredit your earlier responses.

If you wish to make a point about one aspect of your project in the course of this evaluation, but cannot recall the precise detail of the point to which you wish to refer, do not make a vague reference or guess at it; ask if you may directly consult your project so that you can refer to, or quote from, the relevant section.

You should also consider in advance how you can most productively use any time in the oral examination that is given to you for exposition or clarification of your project work. You are most likely to be given such opportunity at the beginning or end of the examination. If it is at the end, and you feel by this stage that you have missed an opportunity to make an important point in answer to an earlier question, then now is the time to do it. Any exposition should consist of more than a simple response to questions already asked. The oral examination is a situation in which further learning about your project work can take place. You should take every opportunity to indicate that the learning process you were involved in did not suddenly cease when you handed in your project.

If you feel, from the questions you are being asked, that the examiners have seriously misunderstood an important aspect of your project, then you should draw attention to this politely, but with conviction, when you have the opportunity. If you feel that they are seriously underestimating some of the real difficulties you encountered when doing the project work then it is your responsibility to politely point this out to the examiners.

Remember throughout that you are a relative expert on the subject matter of your project, since you have been involved closely with it for possibly many months, while the examiners may be relatively unfamiliar with the subject. The additional confidence which this should give you when answering questions should be modified, however, by your appreciation that the people examining you are the experts on the *communication* issues involved.

You should also be sensitive to the circumstances in which the oral examination will take place. Remember, for example, that the external moderator may well have arrived at the venue of the examination after a tiring journey and have had comparatively little time to become familiar with the various projects s/he is to moderate on this occasion. S/he may face the difficult task of getting to grips with the essentials of a number of projects on quite different topics in a short period of time. Your attitude should be that of helping him/her to bring his/her experience to bear upon your work so that you can gain the maximum possible from a constructive criticism of your project. Remember throughout that assessment in the oral is based upon your total understanding of the process of communication your project has involved you in.

ASSIGNMENT X

You should now refer to the end of chapter 4 and complete the following boxes based on your *own* understanding of chapters 5, 6, 7 and 8 of this book:

(F) Communication terms acquired whilst doing project work.

(G) Communication skills acquired whilst doing project work.

(H) Communication concepts relevant to project work.

(I) Communication models relevant to project work.

CASE-STUDY AND PROJECT WORK FOR TEACHERS

9

Introduction

This chapter, intended primarily for the use of teachers, aims firstly to provide some teaching guidelines for approaching and planning case-study and project work; and secondly, some points of connection between the wide range of materials actually used in such work and the communication skills, principles, concepts and models that students need to acquire.

In practice, the basis for the theoretical work is bound to be the student's developing daily experience of communication; and it is this that the teacher has to take account of —and learn from. In this respect the division between teacher and student is bridged, and this chapter may therefore be of some interest to some students, too.

A problem that occurs in books intended as the basis for student activity, such as this one, is raised by Hartley (1979). Reviewing a number of books on simulation as a learning activity, he comments that perhaps

> we now have too many descriptions of activities available and too little comment on their use and evaluation. Which

exercises are most successful with which audience? Which exercises require amendments to suit different groups? What is the most appropriate sequence of exercises to achieve certain objectives? . . . These questions are begged by current literature and left to the individual teacher. This is not very satisfactory given the increasing use of these methods. Are we all doomed to spend our days rediscovering the wheel as we all learn the same lessons the hard way making the same mistakes, using the same original exercises? There is a need for communication here.

The considerable progress that has been made since the early days of teaching communication studies in schools and colleges has come about largely as a result of the initiative and activity of teachers in establishing contacts for the evaluation and exchange of teaching materials. The process evidently needs to continue as the subject develops further.

Case-study work for teachers

Naturally the aim should be that when the chosen case studies have been worked through, the students will have fulfilled the broader requirements of the course. Some syllabuses specify the particular skills, principles, concepts and models of communication that the students should acquire; others are less specific.

While the use of case studies devised by others can provide at least the starting point for such courses, in many cases these will be of only limited local value in stimulating the student's interest in communication theory, and teachers will find it necessary and rewarding to develop their own materials. It is intended that the progression in the complexity of materials included in part one of this book will indicate how

case studies can be built from individual articles, photographs, etc. on a common theme. Theoretically, there would appear to exist an optimum extended case study for each course; in practice (witness the examples included in this book), actual case studies will fall far short of this standard, highlighting some aspects and omitting others. And as the optimum has not yet been discovered — even if it exists — it is necessary for teachers to invent their own case studies.

The good case study should include most of the following ingredients:

(i) The development of necessary skills.
(ii) The application of relevant principles.
(iii) The appreciation and application of relevant concepts.
(iy) The application of relevant communication models.
(v) The basing of the case study upon material which relates closely to other aspects of the communication studies course, e.g. on mass communication, the development of communication and interpersonal communication.

Project work for teachers

Project work attempts to develop the same theoretical understanding of communication as case-study work, but by a different route. There is far more scope here for students to select the material they will work with; and the possibility of more introspection about the process of communication they will experience. It is necessary for the teacher to establish strong connexions between the individual learning activities of students doing project work and the requirements of the syllabus. During the course, the aim of overall development might be sketched as in figure 23.

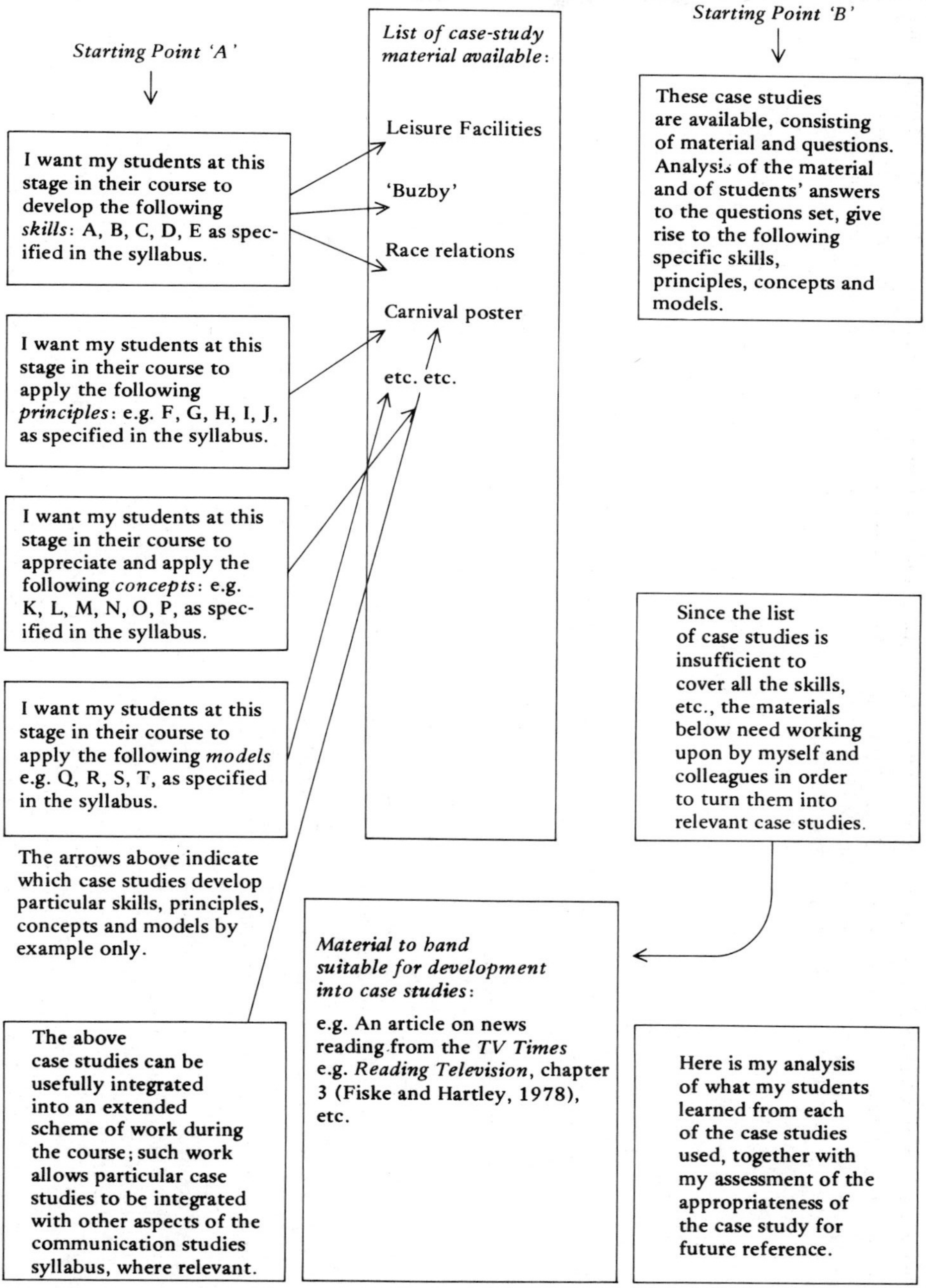

These case studies are available, consisting of material and questions. Analysis of the material and of students' answers to the questions set, give rise to the following specific skills, principles, concepts and models.

Since the list of case studies is insufficient to cover all the skills, etc., the materials below need working upon by myself and colleagues in order to turn them into relevant case studies.

Here is my analysis of what my students learned from each of the case studies used, together with my assessment of the appropriateness of the case study for future reference.

List of case-study material available:

Leisure Facilities

'Buzby'

Race relations

Carnival poster

etc. etc.

Material to band suitable for development into case studies:

e.g. An article on news reading from the *TV Times*

e.g. *Reading Television*, chapter 3 (Fiske and Hartley, 1978),

etc.

I want my students at this stage in their course to *develop* the following *skills*: A, B, C, D, E as specified in the syllabus.

I want my students at this stage in their course to apply the following *principles*: e.g. F, G, H, I, J, as specified in the syllabus.

I want my students at this stage in their course to appreciate and apply the following *concepts*: e.g. K, L, M, N, O, P, as specified in the syllabus.

I want my students at this stage in their course to apply the following *models* e.g. Q, R, S, T, as specified in the syllabus.

The arrows above indicate which case studies develop particular skills, principles, concepts and models by example only.

The above case studies can be usefully integrated into an extended scheme of work during the course; such work allows particular case studies to be integrated with other aspects of the communication studies syllabus, where relevant.

Figure 23 Listing, devising and using case studies: a checklist for teachers

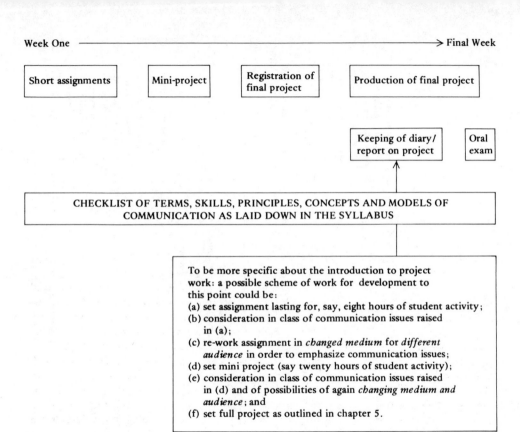

Week One ──────────────────────────────────────→ Final Week

| Short assignments | | Mini-project | | Registration of final project | | Production of final project |

| Keeping of diary/ report on project | | Oral exam |

CHECKLIST OF TERMS, SKILLS, PRINCIPLES, CONCEPTS AND MODELS OF COMMUNICATION AS LAID DOWN IN THE SYLLABUS

To be more specific about the introduction to project work: a possible scheme of work for development to this point could be:
(a) set assignment lasting for, say, eight hours of student activity;
(b) consideration in class of communication issues raised in (a);
(c) re-work assignment in *changed medium* for *different audience* in order to emphasize communication issues;
(d) set mini project (say twenty hours of student activity);
(e) consideration in class of communication issues raised in (d) and of possibilities of again *changing medium and audience*; and
(f) set full project as outlined in chapter 5.

Figure 24

BIBLIOGRAPHY

Introduction

As indicated earlier in the text, there are many writings available which deal, often in a rather abstract manner, with communication theory, and some which deal with the communication skills needed in case-study and project work; but few make any attempt to integrate the two.

This bibliography divides materials by subject matter and by level of experience. The subject areas are: learning to learn; communication skills; communication theory; project work; the mass media. The level of the material is indicated by *S* for students and *T* for teachers.

It is hoped that such signposting will be found useful, but it should be remembered that communication studies is a wide and, ideally, integrated field of study. The divisions made here should in no way be taken as rigid. Progress in learning is evidently made continually by students *and* teachers. Some of the materials included in the mass-media section are relevant to, and could even be in, the theory section; and so on. Some students eventually become teachers and the best teachers are perpetually learning from their students.

Learning to learn

S   Buzan, T. (1981) *Make the Most of Your Mind*, London: Pan Books. A useful physiological approach to the way in which learning performance can be improved. Chapters cover the brain, memory, listening, sight, reading, note-making, fast writing, creativity, numeracy and logic.

T   Rogers, C. R. (1969) *Freedom to Learn*, Columbus: Merrill. Essential background reading for teachers wishing to encourage student activity in project work.

S   Webster, O. (1967) *Read Well and Remember*, London: Pan Books. Includes many comprehension and retention exercises and particularly useful chapters on skimming and aggressive reading.

Communication skills

S   Harding, T. E. (1972) *Let's Write a Script*, Amersham: Hulton Educational Publications. Covers some of the basics of writing scripts for radio and television.

S/T MacShane, D. (1979) *Using the Media*, London: Pluto Press. Aimed at trade unionists and community activists by a former president of the NUJ. A wealth of practical advice — it practises what it preaches.

T   Maine, B. (1939) *The BBC and its Audience*, London: Nelson. A popular, non-theoretical approach to the key notion of audience. Raises practical considerations from the viewpoint of the BBC at a time when it enjoyed its monopoly in broadcasting.

T   Management Games Ltd. 'Radio Covingham'. Simulation useful for practice of skills and for reflection on local radio. A description and evaluation of this simulation is included in M. Alvarado, 'Simulation as a method', *Screen Education*, 14 (Spring 1975).

T   Maude, B. (1974) *Practical Communication for Managers*, London: Longman. Relates communication skills used in industrial situations to some aspects of communication theory.

T   Read, H. (1972) *Communication Methods for All Media*, Illinois: University of Illinois Press. Defines and gives some useful examples of some skills and elements within the communication process. Some of its comments remain vague and too tied to US culture.

T   Taylor, J. L. and Walford, R. (1972) *Simulation in the Classroom*, Harmondsworth: Penguin. Useful introduction as basis for role play in case-study work. Contains 'Front Page' which gives students chance to edit a local newspaper and to reflect on decisions taken.

Communication theory

S/T Argyle, M. (1972) *The Psychology of Interpersonal Behaviour*, Harmondsworth: Penguin. Good introduction to non-verbal behaviour.

S/T Berger, J. (1972) *Ways of Seeing*, Harmondsworth: Penguin and BBC. Dramatic critique of the way visual images are employed in popular culture. Based on a television series.

S/T Blake, R. H. and Haroldson, E. O. (1975) *A Taxonomy of Concepts in Communication*, New York: Hastings House. Useful exposition of communication terms with detailed cross references and some brief examples.

T   Buckhout, T. (1900) Eyewitness testimony in 'Readings from the Scientific American'. Demonstrates how easily eye witnesses can be guilty of perceptual errors by describing a number of experiments in detail.

S/T Cardiff, D., Cram, D. and Dyer, G. (1973) 'The broadcast interview', Polytechnic of Central London. An unpublished paper suggesting a number of possible frameworks for analysing what goes on in interviews. Useful preliminary reading for students doing interviews during project work.

T   Caughie, J. (ed.) (1978) *Television: Ideology and Exchange*, London: British Film Institute. Essays directed at examining how television exerts its ideological influence.

T   Cherry, C. (1957) *On Human Communication*, Cambridge, Mass.: MIT Press. Fundamental work on communication theory with useful glossary.

S/T Cohen, S. and Young, J. (1973) *The Manufacture of News*, London: Constable. Essays by various hands on how the mass media treats social problems, minorities and deviancy.

T   Corner, J. and Hawthorn, J. (1980) *Communication*

Studies: An Introductory Reader, London: Edward Arnold. Useful source book of sometimes difficult readings on communication theory. Each extract is introduced by the authors.

T Dennett, T. and Spence, J. (1976/7) 'Photography, ideology and education', *Screen Education*, 21 (Winter 1976/7). Suggests some practical ways in which the concept of ideology can be clarified through the study of photography.

T Evans, H. (1978) *Pictures on a Page*, London: Heinemann. Examples of how photography is used in the press by a former editor of *The Times*. Compared with Berger, however, an incidental rather than fundamental critique of current practices.

S/T Fiske, J. (1982) *Introduction to Communication Studies*, London: Methuen. A good introduction to this series.

T Freire, P. (1972) *Pedagogy of the Oppressed*, Harmondsworth: Penguin. Complex presentation of the thesis that education is never ideology free. Argues positively that education can help to change the world.

T Gauthier, G. (1976) *The Semiology of the Image*, London: British Film Institute Advisory Document. Suggests useful ideas for presentation of images in class. Accompanying slides available from the British Film Institute.

T Lowndes, D. (1976) 'The Unesco survey and the British situation', *Screen Education*, 18. Argues that a purely liberal approach to studying the mass media is inadequate to defend children while the resources of education are dwarfed by media power.

T McQuail, D. (1975) *Communication*, London: Longman. A generally difficult and abstract approach to theory, contains some useful insights but too many qualifications of the points it makes.

T Parry, J. (1967) *The Psychology of Human Communication*, London: University of London Press. Some chapters, such as the one on barriers, are useful for reference and exposition to class.

S/T Richards, I. A. (1929) *Practical Criticism*, London: Routledge & Kegan Paul. Practical approach to literary criticism: 'the one and only goal of all critical endeavours, of all interpretation, appreciation, exhortation, praise or abuse, is improvement in communication'.

T Scheflor, A. E. (1972) *Body Language and the Social Order*, Englewood Cliffs, NJ: Prentice Hall. Introduction to kinesics; useful illustrations, difficult language.

T Schools Council (1978) *Startline: Schools Council Moral Education 8–13 Project*, London: Longmans and Schools Council. Contains posters and photographs aimed at increasing 'children's awareness of the verbal and non-verbal aspects of behaviour'. Useful for wider groups than the title suggests.

S/T Vernon, M. D. (1972) *The Psychology of Perception*, Harmondsworth: Pelican. Systematically introduces problems of perception, with illustrations which can be used in class.

Project work

S Hare, R. (1970) *Know-How — A Student's Guide to Project Work*, London: International Textbook Cc. Ltd. A useful guide to the practical and technical elements in project work. Sections on organizing projects, research, interviewing, tape-recorders, cameras, etc. but does not in general relate these to theoretical issues.

S   Parsons, D. J. (1972) *Theses and Project Work*, London: Allen & Unwin. Deals with appropriate ways of presenting the written project and includes chapters on organization and research. Many of the comments are aimed at under- or post-graduate students.

T   Scottish Education Department, Central Committee on English, Central Project Group (1970) *Projects in Practice*, Edinburgh: HMSO. Gives some indication of the value of project work in developing language skills amongst school students.

Mass media

S/T   Bakewell, J. and Garnham, N. (1970) *The New Priesthood*, London: Allen Lane. Useful behind-the-scenes look at the people who control and produce what we see on television.

T   Beharell, P. and Philo, G. (eds.) (1977) *Trade Unions and the Media*, London: Macmillan. Collection of essays discussing the generally poor image of trade unions conveyed by the mass media.

T   BBC (1971) *News Broadcasting and the Public*, London: BBC. Dated, but includes useful data on audience attitudes to television news.

S/T   Curran, J., Gurevitch, M. and Woollacott, J. (1977) *Mass Communication and Society*, London: Edward Arnold. Stimulating and wide-ranging collection of essays by various hands, prepared for the Open University.

S/T   Fiske, J. and Hartley, J. (1978) *Reading Television*, London: Methuen. Analyses how television operates within our culture.

T   *Future of Broadcasting*. Committee Report, Chairman: Lord Annan, London: HMSO. Such government commissioned reports are useful for factual information if nothing else. This one's Open Broadcasting Authority proposals have now been overtaken by events, but may yet influence the future.

S/T   Gardner, C. (ed.) (1979) *Media Politics and Culture: A Socialist View*, London: Macmillan. Collection of essays offering critique of existing media practice and suggesting alternatives.

S/T   Glasgow University Media Group (1976) *Bad News*, vol. 1, London: Routledge & Kegan Paul. Surveys six months of industrial news on television, concluding that this medium tends to lay the blame for society's economic problems at the door of the workforce. A video version of the book's main points is also available.

S/T   Groombridge, B. (1972) *Television and the People*, Harmondsworth: Penguin. Short but stimulating, it explains the practices of television and argues for changes to allow greater public participation.

S/T   Halloran, J. D., Murdock, G. and Elliott, P. (1970) *Demonstrations and Communications: A Case Study*, Harmondsworth: Penguin. Analyses newspaper and television coverage of a demonstration against US policy in Vietnam. Shows how presentation of events which occurred tended to be fitted into a formula established earlier by the media.

S/T   Hoggart, R. (1970) *Speaking to Each Other, vol. 1: About Literature*, London: Chatto & Windus. Essential on the inadequacies of the traditional techniques of literary criticism and on the necessity to establish alternatives which can illuminate mass-media practice.

S/T McQuail, D. (ed.) (1972) *Sociology of Mass Communications*, Harmondsworth: Penguin. Twenty essays by various hands covering a substantial part of the field.

S/T Mander, J. (1980) *Four Arguments for the Elimination of Television*, Brighton: Harvester Press. 'The role of television is to project that world, via changes, into our heads, all of us at the same time'. Essential reading.

T Masterman, L. (1980) *Teaching About Television*, London: Macmillan. A mine of information and ideas; its greatest strength, amongst many, is that they arise from classroom practice.

S/T *Media Reporter*, Derby: Brennan Publications. A valuable quarterly review, aimed primarily at media practitioners and theorists.

S/T Scupham, J. (1970) *The Revolution in Communications*, New York: Holt, Rhinehart & Winston. Written by a former controller of the BBC, its approach is a useful counterpoint to the prevailing left-wing origin of UK media theory.

T Smith, A. (1976) *The Shadow in the Cave*, New York: Quartet. Thought provoking contribution to the debate on the future of broadcasting.

T Smith, A. C. H. (1975) *The Popular Press and Social Change*, London: Chatto & Windus. Demonstrates well how detailed investigations of particular newspapers can provide the basis for wider conclusions.

T Tunstall, J. (ed.) (1973) *Media Sociology*, Constable. Introductory reading on the sociology of the mass media.

S/T Williams, R. (1975) *Communications*, Harmondsworth: Penguin. Pioneering work, its analysis of press content indicates how to navigate some choppy seas.

T Willis, P. (1979) 'What is news? A case study'. *Working Papers in Cultural Studies*, 1. Covers 'bias' in news presentations.

REFERENCES

Alderson, C. (1968) *Magazines Teenagers Read*, London: Pergamon.

Associated Examining Board (1977/1978/1980/1984) *Communication Studies at Advanced Level* (syllabus, specimen case study, registered projects), Aldershot, Hants: Associated Examining Board.

Baggaley, J. and Duck, S. (1976) *The Dynamics of Television*, Farnborough, Hants: Saxon House.

Barnlund, D.C. (1968) *Interpersonal Communication: Survey and Studies*, Boston, Mass.: Houghton Mifflin.

Benn (1982) *Press Directory*, UK, Tunbridge Wells: Benn Publications.

Berelson, B. and Steiner, G. A. (1964) *Human Behaviour*, New York: Harcourt, Brace & World.

Berger, J. (1972) *Ways of Seeing*, London: BBC and Penguin Books.

Berlo, D. K. (1960) *The Process of Communication*, New York: Holt, Rinehart & Winston.

Bernstein, B. (1973) *Class, Codes and Control*, London: Paladin.

Blake, R. H. and Haroldsen, E. O. (1975) *A Taxonomy of Concepts in Communication*, New York: Hastings House.

Buzan, T. (1981) *Make the Most of Your Mind*, London: Pan Books.

Chandor, P. (1950) *Advertising and Publicity*, London: English Universities Press.

Cherry, C. (1966, 1st ed. 1957) *On Human Communication*, Cambridge, Mass.: MIT Press.

Corner, J. and Hawthorn, J. (1980) *Communication Studies: An Introductory Reader*, London: Edward Arnold.

Danby, J. F. (1949) *Shakespeare's Doctrine of Nature*, London: Faber.

Dixon, J. with Brown, J. and Barnes, D. (1979) *Education 16–19: The Role of English and Communication*, London: Macmillan.

Dyer, G. (1982) *Advertising as Communication*, London: Methuen.

Evans, H. (1978) *Pictures on a Page*, London: Heinemann.

Fiske, J. (1982) *Introduction to Communication Studies*, London: Methuen.

Gallwey, W. T. (1975) *The Inner Game of Tennis*, London: Cape.

Gerbner, G. (1956) 'Toward a general model of communication' in *Audio Visual Communication Review*, IV: 3, pp. 171–99.

Glasgow University Media Group (1976) *Bad News*, London: Routledge & Kegan Paul.

Golding, P. (1974) *The Mass Media*, London: Longman.

Gramsci, A. (1971) *Prison Notebooks*, London: Lawrence & Wishart.

Hare, R. (1970) *Know-How: A Student's Guide to Project Work*, London: International Textbook Co.

Hartley, J. (1982) *Understanding News*, London: Methuen.

Hartley, P. (1979) 'Games we all play', in *Communication Studies Bulletin* 5, Sheffield: Department of Communication Studies, Sheffield City Polytechnic.

Hartmann, P. and Husband, C. (1971) 'The mass media and racial conflict', in S. Cohen and J. Young (eds), *The Manufacture of News*, London: Constable.

Hayakawa, S. (1974) *Language in Thought and Action*, London: Allen & Unwin.

Hills, P. J. (1979) *Teaching and Learning as a Communication Process*, London: Croom Helm.

Hoare, Q. and Nowell Smith, G. (1971) *Selections from the Prison Notebooks of Antonio Gramsci*, London: Lawrence & Wishart.

Hoebel, E. A. (1966) *Anthropology: The Study of Man*, New York: McGraw Hill.

Hoggart, R. (1970) *Speaking to Each Other: About Literature*, London: Chatto & Windus.

Irvine Smith, R. (1968) *Men and Societies*, London: Heinemann.

Lasswell, H. D. (1948) 'The structure and function of communication in society', in L. Bryson (ed.), *The Communication of Ideas*, New York: Harper & Row.

Leach, E. (1976) *Culture and Communication*, Cambridge: Cambridge University Press.

Mack, J. (1978) 'Education in the media', in *New Society*, 2 November.

McQuail, D. (ed.) (1972) *Sociology of Mass Communications*, Harmondsworth: Penguin.

MacShane, D. (1979) *Using the Media: How to Deal with the Press, Television and Radio*, London: Pluto Press.

Masterman, L. (1980) *Teaching About Television*, London: Macmillan.

Mortensen, C. D. and Schneider, M. (1972) *Explorations in Communication*, New York: McGraw Hill.

Osgood, C. (1967) *The Measurement of Meaning*, Urbana, Illinois: University of Illinois Press.

Parry, J. (1967) *The Psychology of Human Communication*, London: University of London Press.

Peddiwell, J. A. (1939) *The Sabre-Tooth Curriculum*, New York: McGraw Hill.

Pirsig, R. M. (1976) *Zen and the Art of Motorcycle Maintenance*, London: Corgi (first published by Bodley Head, 1974).

Plaskow, M. and Stuart, D. (1979) *New Directions in Communication Studies*, BBC Radio Four Discussion, 'The World Tonight', 24 May, London: BBC.

Ross, R. S. (1965) *Speech Communication: Fundamentals and Practice*, New Jersey: Prentice Hall.

Roszak, T. (1970) *The Making of a Counter Culture*, London: Faber.

Sansom, W. (1972) *Birth of a Novel*, London: Hutchinson.

Schools Council (1977) *Opportunities for Writing at Seventeen Plus*, Leeds: The Schools Council.

Schools Council (1978) *Communication Studies: B — The First Term*, Leeds: Schools Council.

Schramm, W. (ed.) (1960) *Mass Communications*, Urbana, Illinois: University of Illinois Press.

Shannon, C. and Weaver, W. C. (1949) *The Mathematical Theory of Communication*, Urbana, Illinois: University of Illinois Press.

Shibutani, T. (1966) *Improvised News: A Sociological Study of Rumour*, Indianapolis, Indiana: Bobbs-Merrill.

Vidal, G. (1976) *1876: A Novel*, London: Heinemann.

Weiss, P. (1968) 'The necessary decision', in *New Left Review* 47, pp. 31–8.

Westley, B. H. and MacLean, M. S. Jr. (1957) 'A conceptual model of communication research, in *Journalism Quarterly* 34.